Katamari Damacy

L. E. Hall

Boss Fight Books
Los Angeles, CA
bossfightbooks.com

Copyright © 2018 L. E. Hall
All rights reserved.

ISBN 13: 978-1940535-17-3
First Printing: 2018

Series Editor: Gabe Durham
Book Design by Ken Baumann & Cory Schmitz
Page Design by Christopher Moyer

Katamari Damacy

For my parents, and especially my sister

CONTENTS

WHAT IN THE WORLD
IS A KATAMARI?

The katamari. The Prince.
Where the first rolls the second follows.
Roll, roll, roll.

— The King of All Cosmos

FROM YOUR VERY FIRST encounter with *Katamari Damacy*, you're being taught how to play it.

When you first load it on the PlayStation 2, you're greeted by the Namco logo on a white screen, and the sound of a man humming and singing a theme tune that will soon become very familiar: "*Nah... nah nah nah nah nah nah nah.*"

A tiny, hammer-headed green figure, the Prince of All Cosmos, stands behind a lumpy pink and yellow ball: a *katamari*. The player controls the Prince's (and the katamari's) direction with the PlayStation 2 thumbsticks, moving left to right, or rolling forward, accompanied by what sounds like the squeak of a rubber dog toy. Pushing the sticks forward causes the Prince to roll the sticky katamari toward the letters of Namco. It rolls over the logo, taking a piece with it as it continues toward the distant horizon, and in doing so, loads a saved game or begins a new one.

Just one screen into the game and you already have a sense of the physicality of *Katamari Damacy*. You understand how you, the Prince, and the katamari interact with objects in this world. The gameplay itself has assimilated the text on the title screen—and thus the external "meta" world—into the game world, hinting at the fun yet to come.

The man's humming turns into a growing chorus as the screen shifts to a pastoral scene of cartoon cows grazing against a blue sky. A dark, strangely-shaped figure rises on the horizon as the game title appears: *Katamari Damacy*, a name that in Japanese (*Katamari Damashii*) translates to "lump of souls" or "clump of spirits."

Two rainbow spotlights burst onto the screen, revealing the King of All Cosmos, an impressively mustachioed man with a sparkling, crown-bedecked purple hammer-head. He's decked out in a giant ruffled collar and gold neck chain, tights beneath his billowing purple cape, and a skin-tight muscle shirt that shows off his royal gym body.

The joyous abandon begins as the King takes off into the sky above Mount Fuji. A crane flaps by, holding the

Prince in a little swing hanging from its beak. Another crane flies by, clutching a turtle. Why not!

Four duck heads pop into frame, singing along with the theme tune. Four more appear on the opposite side, joining in, as giraffes and elephants dance in front of the mountain. It's an ecstatic song with bright horns and thumping drums. A rainbow fills the screen, which the Prince slides down on his way to hang out with his family, the King and Queen. The King plays a guitar while the tiny Prince dances on his knee; the Queen, resplendent in pink and white, looks on adoringly.

The camera cuts the King flying over the land, sending sparkles down on dancing pandas, flowers, mushrooms, butterflies, and other animals. The scene closes with the King and his family driving in a convertible down a mushroom-speckled lane towards a huge castle in the clouds, under the bright arches of a rainbow.

This is the world of *Katamari Damacy*: bright, loud, and joyfully absurd. The game's scale can be as small as a turtle or as massive as the entire universe. Either way, you're happy to be along for the ride.

MAKE A STAR

And oh, We have an idea.
If the katamari is large enough,
We'll be sure to turn it into a star.

—The King of All Cosmos

IF I WERE TO ASK YOU, "What is *Katamari Damacy* about?", it would be no surprise if you started telling me about the game's goofy plot: A tiny, hammer-headed Prince is sent to Earth on a mission to reconstruct the night sky after his father, the bossy King of All Cosmos, destroyed all of the stars on a drunken bender. "*Katamari*," you might tell me, "is a game about putting the stars back together again."

But what *Katamari* is really about is *how* you form those stars: by rolling a sticky, bumpy ball around and picking up objects as you run into them. You and the ball are controlled by the two analog thumb sticks on the PlayStation 2 controller. Push both forward to go forward, or push one back and one forward to turn.

That simple mechanic, hinted at in the game's opening screen, is at the core of all the fun to follow.

As the five-centimeter-high Prince, you begin the first level, "Make a Star 1," in an ordinary Japanese home, on a tabletop littered with small objects like thumbtacks, dice, stamps, matches, and erasers. The art style is blocky and childlike, and rendered with a cartoony economy of detail that imbues the objects with humor.

The bowls, teapots, and cans of condensed milk surrounding you are massive compared to you and your katamari's current size. But with each object that's added to it, the katamari grows. And the larger the katamari gets, the bigger the objects that will stick to it.

For now you are confined to the living room of the house, with potential objects to roll up generally adhering to things you might find in a regular home: pushpins, memory cards, pencils. Everything has a fairly simplistic geometry, although some objects are longer or bulkier than others.

By rolling around and either picking up or colliding with objects, the player quickly gets a sense of what things are likely to stick to the katamari at a given size, versus which things they'll merely bounce off of. Generally, much larger objects, such as phones or books, form part of the level environment, providing barrier walls or ramps from low to high areas.

Growing in scale as you pick up objects, you roll off the table, and begin to move around the floor. Larger things, like lipsticks, batteries, coins, ping pong balls, and mahjong tiles, begin to stick to your katamari. All around you are animal obstacles, including snails and butterflies; getting too close to one sounds a warning alarm.

Rolling your katamari over a small object picks it up with a satisfying *sproing*-y noise, but collide with an object that's too big for you and a few pieces will drop off of your katamari, reducing its size. If the oversized object is one of those animal obstacles, it can knock you off course, scattering your katamari pieces. But if you're *almost* big enough to roll it up, the animal will bounce and fall away from you, momentarily stunned. Later, you can do this to humans on the street, who will scream and run away from you as you chase them down, a cartoonish reaction that's more funny than frightening.

You eventually learn to test whether smaller objects are the right size for collecting by colliding with them. When an object appears to be a likely candidate, but is slightly too big for the katamari to pick up, it wiggles when the katamari hits it, and the controller vibrates. Often this interaction proves to be a fun challenge, as players scout nearby for other, smaller objects they *can* collect, in order to roll up the tantalizingly close item, which has taken on a new desirability.

Once your katamari has reached ten centimeters in size (roughly the size of an in-game cucumber), the screen shimmers for a moment as the camera angle adjusts to be slightly higher and farther back. Now you're able to roll past the house's barriers and out into the garden, where you encounter more objects like dandelions, pairs of glasses, paintbrushes, vegetables, magnets, plates of chicken drumsticks, and more.

When you're in the house and garden levels, the objects you encounter are fairly commonplace, like food, books, or clothing. Nothing ever feels completely out of place, although they're sometimes playfully absurd in their placement or arrangement—a massive stack of piggy banks, for example, or a row of golf balls that also contains one bird egg.

Returning to the house after some time clearing the garden, you're now significantly larger, which lets you roll back up to the same tabletop surface where you started. Now, however, you can swallow up the teapots and bowls that loomed so large earlier, as well as emerald rings, teacups, canned pineapple, tape dispensers, and a mouse named Gerald.

The sheer number and range of objects that you encounter in *Katamari Damacy* is charming in and of itself. But their placement is sometimes random, and their juxtaposition with other elements can be unexpectedly whimsical: Only in *Katamari* could you encounter a mouse carrying a tray of *takoyaki*, a Japanese snack of wheat batter balls with an octopus filling. And you continue to discover new objects and re-encounter familiar objects you're newly able to roll up, making for a dynamic and ever-changing experience.

The wondrous feeling increases as you progress through the game and your katamari grows larger and more formidable. Rolling out of the house, you later find yourself on a city street, scooping up penguins, shop signs, boomboxes, and high school students, in the shadows of objects like a boulder-sized *daruma* figurine or a tree-sized mushroom. Eventually, the junk-laden ball is large enough for the King to toss it back up into the night sky to be transformed into a star or constellation, restoring a small piece of the cosmos he wrecked. Ultimately everything, from the smallest accessory to the walls, city streets, and houses that were once fencing you in, is an object to be absorbed into your great sticky ball.

It's not always easy to collect all the items you need to grow your katamari, but it's never confusing. Levels may have time limits or specific challenges, but the worst thing that happens if you don't meet your goal is that you get stern scolding from the King.

Even as video game technology has advanced so much since the game's release, *Katamari Damacy* stands out today because it offers us a type of play more common to children on a playground—something uniquely internal and almost anarchic. It's like building a tower of blocks just for the sheer joy of pushing it down.

KEITA'S MIXED MEDIA

Beyond comprehension.
A thing of wonder.

—The King of All Cosmos

KATAMARI CREATOR KEITA TAKAHASHI has always had a strong, unapologetic sense of his own artistic vision. Born in 1975 in Kitakyūshū, Japan, to a math-loving homemaker and deep-sea salvage expert, he and his two sisters were actively encouraged in their creative pursuits.

"I started to go to art class when I was around four or five years old in Japan," Takahashi told me in an interview. "It was so fun." He was drawn to the variety of crafts, like painting, clay, woodcut, paper cut-out, and pottery. "So I got into making and drawing. I became interested in architecture when I was at middle school."

Takahashi has always been interested in the domestic sphere, and the realm of objects and spaces used by ordinary people during their daily lives. He wasn't interested in large, flashy skyscrapers or elaborate concert halls, preferring instead to think about designing "small houses for common families, because houses are one of the necessities of modern life."

However, where he lived, the houses were all similar to one another, and even at a young age he found the repetitiveness of the designs boring.

"Also, I thought being an architect must be a stable job, because it's one of the necessities of modern life," he added. "But I gave up before trying it out because the exam for the architecture course required mathematics."

Takahashi had a variety of hobbies and participated in a number of extracurricular activities upon reaching high school, including being a member of the rugby club. But despite having left behind his dream of becoming an architect, he still felt drawn to the pursuit of art.

In Japan, it's common for high school students and graduates to enroll in evening or weekend *juku,* or "cram schools," which focus intensely on single subjects, to prepare them for the country's competitive university entrance exams. Takahashi enrolled at an art-focused *juku* to learn the basics of the medium and develop his skills.

"I studied basic design at that art cram school," he said. "I did collage, pencil-drawing, color compositions, et cetera, in that class, but it wasn't interesting. So I changed my subject at art cram school from basic design to sculpture, because I remembered the fun time I had making something with clay at my first art class as a kid. And that change was correct."

Takahashi quickly found himself drawn to the tangible nature of working with physical materials. Sculpting with clay and drawing with charcoal were "very simple" on the surface but required a lot of skill.

"Making things you can actually touch was more impressive than just painting something," he said. "And you know, they don't use any 'color' in sculpture class. Clay is gray, charcoal is black, and paper is white. But I could find many colors and depth between gray, black and white, and light and shadow. Simple, but deep."

With these skills in hand, Takahashi was prepared to enter university. But he knew his artistic exploration was just beginning.

"Learning sculpture was good, but I didn't care what sculpture should be," he said. "Just making actual physical stuff was fun to me. I knew that even though I could [major in] sculpture [as a] subject at art university, it would be harder to get a job after graduating, than [if I had studied] design in general. I didn't know what I wanted to make at university. Art cram school teachers provided us very specific assignments every week or two, so I just did what they said. But at university, you have to make [this formal thing] called 'sculpture' by yourself."

"I was thinking about this before I entered university," he added. "It sounds silly, but I did. *What should I make there? How do I sustain my life by making sculptures?*"

In 1995, Takahashi was admitted into Musashino Art University, a highly-regarded school for art and design based in Kodaira, a city in western Tokyo. Notable alumni include manga artist and anime director Satoshi Kon, art director of MUJI Kenya Hara, and the designer of Hello Kitty, Yuko Shimizu.

Around the time of his second year at university, he started to gain a sense of clarity. And as his creative process developed, the philosophies that would advise the rest of his collegiate work began to emerge.

"*What should I create? And what kind of meaning is there inherent in sculpture?*" he recalled wondering, in a postmortem of *Katamari Damacy* delivered at the Game Developers Conference (GDC) in 2005. He described a tension in trying to compare man-made sculptures and artworks to things in nature, like "plants, trees, flowers, mountains, oceans," describing them as "much more beautiful than what people can create." Further, he felt that many ideas expressed in artwork "[tend] to be so highbrow that people cannot really understand [them]."

And what is the point of formal, gallery-bound, capital-A "Art," he wondered, if it's isn't beautiful, practical, helpful to humanity, or even understandable?

"Making sculpture or art is very useless [to the world] compared to other jobs like doctors, teachers, or farmers," he told me. "If there was a ranking board of job importance, sculptor definitely would be very low-ranked. Also, if I just made a typical sculpture, even though everyone loves it, you might have to go to a gallery or a museum to see it. When you feel hungry, food is much more important than great art. So that also made me think that art is so useless! But unfortunately, I like to make things. So I had to find an answer for myself."

Takahashi describes his perspective as extreme, but his answer to this difficult question came when he discovered another possibility: He could make art that was both useful and accessible.

"I just thought, 'What if I use these as "ordinary tools"—maybe I can keep having and using them after I've finished making it?' That means, stuff that I make will have functional elements," he said. "I started with that conclusion first, and that worked very well."

This philosophy is apparent in the art that Takahashi created during his time at Musashino University, which focused on mixing the whimsical with the practical.

"I found that a small amount of humor makes people smile," he said. "And I actually felt that was more of a big deal than having a function as a tool. So at university I focused on how to make things a bit funny, but also kinda functional or practical. Something that makes people smile, but that shouldn't be 'Art.' Maybe ordinary things or tools that you can buy at Target or Home Depot."

The objects included a *chabudai*, a traditional short-legged, collapsible table that transformed into a robot; a figure of a goat with a flower pot in its back, allowing excess water to drain through its udders; and woven garbage cans with rounded bottoms that continually rock back and forth.

There was also a hippo that served as the cover of a tissue box, a play on words: The Japanese word for hippo is *kaba*, which sounds similar to *kabā*, the Japanese phonetic pronunciation of the English word "cover."

Another, entitled "Glove Box," was a jointed, near life-size figure of a disgruntled man in an orange space suit, with a small door in his chest that swings open to reveal a small shelf space. Part of the comedy of the piece is the way the function of the shelf is subsumed by the spaceman himself. No matter what you put inside guy's chest cavity, you've still got to figure out what to do with the enormous, surly spaceman.

The objects themselves are beautifully and realistically rendered, but each one has something surprising about it, a small detail or feature designed to provoke a smile or a laugh.

During the GDC 2005 postmortem, Takahashi showed off pictures of his creations, describing their functions and what they meant to him. Of the robot table, he said: "[I]t can't change forms on its own—you need two people to be able to change its form, so it's actually a beautiful communication tool."

In art school, Takahashi felt that he didn't quite fit in with his fellow students, whose work he didn't care for. He was also bothered by their wastefulness.

"Some of them threw away what they made into a dumpster," he said. "I really hated it."

At GDC 2005, Takahashi reflected on the formal fine arts scene, and how those types of creators are typically perceived by society.

"It's just as though the artists are really excited about it themselves," he said. "People who are artists and writers are certainly admired, but I always wondered if they really are contributing anything to society. The artists will say, 'I understand the value of what I'm making—I am great,' but it might be just all in that person's head. So that never sat well with me. I was young and perhaps I was too pure. But I couldn't see how sculpture can tie into our lives."

This strategy of merging philosophy and function is fundamental to Takahashi's work. It reflects his perception of the world as an interconnected, functioning, fundamentally hopeful entity.

During that speech, Takahashi spoke about working to figure out how he could make expressive art that was also relevant and connected to the larger world, something that spoke to the issues we all share:

> All around us, we have trash; we have trash problems. We have the problems of an oil crisis. All around the world there are battles. And there are also tons of problems even closer to home. But I was trying to think, as an individual, how I can deal, how I can contribute to something like that? And I just kept wondering what on earth I was doing. During these two or three years, I kept thinking about that constantly.

> What I came up with is very simple. I thought I would like to do something that makes people happy. It's so simple that you might think I really didn't give it much thought. But at that time, I thought that if a person could be happy or laugh even just a little bit, even for a moment, then they won't rush off to work and people and countries will perhaps stop fighting and do these unnecessary battles. And in an extreme sense, perhaps this might lead to lack of racial discrimination and wars.

Takahashi dreamed of world without trash, conflict, or hatred—a world where all of nature and civilization could be a beautiful, diverse clump of souls.

•

After graduating from Musashino, Takahashi knew he needed a job, but wasn't interested in pursuing life as a sculptor.

"I preferred to work as a designer rather than an artist, if that was possible," he said. "So I was looking for a job that makes something fun, commercially, and I found the video game industry."

Although Takahashi hadn't played many games at university, he had played a lot of video games as a kid, and was particularly fond of Nintendo's offerings. "I used to enjoy the Famicom era very much," he told Gamasutra's Simon Parkin in 2009. "In fact, at that time I was overweight because I played so many games."

"I still remember playing mainstream titles like *Dragon Quest* and *Final Fantasy*," he said in a 2008 interview at IndieCade. "I can't help but remember because I was so caught up with leveling up my characters."

Takahashi was excited about the idea of working in an art form that reached a wide audience in the way that games had once reached him.

"[M]aking things was more fun than just playing video games that someone else had made," he told me. "I knew that video games were a very popular entertainment in the world. You can buy games from game shops in any country. That's easier than going to an art museum. And video games are a medium that have a strong and intuitive interactivity, more than anything else. I still think the interactivity of video games is kind of a miracle."

At the time, the Japanese economy was experiencing a period of extreme instability. Now known as the "Lost Decade," the period from 1991 to at least 2000 saw a significant decline in the country's GDP and wages after the burst of an enormous speculative asset price bubble. All of the major Japanese game studios reported declining profits, and were growing increasingly concerned with how to stay afloat.

Anticipating the introduction of new, NASDAQ-like Japanese stock exchanges scheduled for 1999, Konami, Namco, and Sega all made moves to divide their companies into smaller subsidiaries with the hope that these smaller nodes would be capable of attracting venture capital to speed up the development of new video game titles.

In 1997, Konami had created a technology development center, Konami Computer Entertainment School. In the following years, the school saw great success in nurturing, and subsequently hiring, many of the young, talented game designers that passed through the program. Its affiliated development studio, Konami Games & Music Division (later, Bemani) was responsible for a string of hit games, including *Beatmania* in 1997, and both *Dance Dance Revolution* and *GuitarFreaks* in 1998, resulting in significant profits for the company. The other major studios took note.

In 1999, Namco recorded a sharp drop in sales and profit for the year. Ascribing it to "lower income from its amusement centers and lack of hit consumer software," the company underwent its own period of dividing itself into smaller operations, shutting down unprofitable arcades, and creating research and development labs to encourage the creation of higher-quality content, in the style of the Konami education program.

Namco also underwent a restructuring program, closing fifteen sales offices in Japan to increase the amusement division's gross operating margin from 8% to 15%. The closure of the sales offices was designed to save approximately two billion yen per year, while a simultaneous 10% reduction in the number of arcades run by the company (at that time, 450 locations) would improve earnings by three to four million yen.

It was in the midst of this tumultuous environment that Takahashi joined the video game industry. And although nobody knew it at the time, this growing trend of studio-based game creation would be essential to the future existence of *Katamari Damacy*.

•

At Namco, Takahashi saw an opportunity to further expand his skill set, and to explore the potential of a new medium.

"I wanted to try a new thing, and see how much I could do at a new pace," he said. "At university, the things I did were almost all physical 3D stuff, but video games are 2D—meaning, on a TV screen. Less physical, and also 100% digital. I didn't have any consoles or computers. I didn't know how to use Adobe stuff or 3D modeling tools until I joined Namco."

The video game industry also offered new opportunities for collaboration.

"I wanted to try to work with many people as a way of gaining life experience because making things at university was solo work," he said. "And I knew video games are kinda similar to sculpture—because, to me, both are fun but useless. Like I was thinking about before entering university, I was also considering what kind of video games I should make before I joined Namco. I applied for a job as a 3D artist, though."

Takahashi chose Namco because he had enjoyed many of their games when he was younger, including *Sky Kid*, *Dig Dug*, *Mappy*, *The Tower of Druaga*, *Metro-Cross*, and *Pac-Man*.

"I think almost all the old Namco games I liked were very unique and very well-made," he said. "So I just picked Namco by my sweet memories."

He had some qualms about the company's more recent games, though.

"I felt that the games Namco had developed around 1999 were typical [of games at the time]," he said. "1999 was just one year before the launch of the PlayStation 2. For me, they looked like they were focused on making 3D polygon games that didn't have any sense of humor: *Ridge Racer*, *Tekken*, *Time Crisis*, *Soulcalibur*, and the Tales series. I know initially some Tales series were not 3D polygon games, but I was shocked by the fact that Namco made that sort of JRPG. That Namco was so different from my old sweet Namco."

Takahashi was disappointed enough in Namco's current games that he brought it up in his job interview, asking the interviewers, "Why does Namco need to make *Tales of Phantasia*? Because that game doesn't look like a Namco game, to me."

"They just laughed," he later said of the interview, "but I think they understood what I wanted to say."

Takahashi's unconventional, uncompromising approach proved to be both a challenge and a virtue.

"The first step of the process of joining Namco was a portfolio test, and a small drawing test," he said. "I just showed what I made at university and drew something cute, I guess. And I passed the first test. The second step was an interview with senior artists, and I asked that [same] question [about Namco making *Tales of*

Phantasia], and I passed it. Then the last thing was an interview with executives, and I failed."

Luckily for all future fans of *Katamari*, that wasn't the end of the road.

"Actually, I found out the funny truth after I joined Namco, from an HR guy who I got along with," Takahashi said. "I failed the last job interview for sure. Sounds like some executives didn't like me. But one of the interviewers from the artist interview persuaded an executive who was his boss to hire me. So I asked him, 'Why?' He said, 'You looked very unique, and I felt there was potential to make something fun with you.'"

Upon joining Namco, Takahashi was given a six-month training period. He spent the first two months working in an actual arcade and the next two learning digital tools, 3D modeling, texture mapping, and other game-making skills. The team used a Silicon Graphics workstation for the now-discontinued Softimage 3D modeling tool, and a Mac for Photoshop.

In his 2008 interview at IndieCade, Takahashi talked about approaching the video game industry as a new, untested creator.

"During that time, I had no idea what was involved in making a game —the process, et cetera. It was a learning experience every day for me. Since test projects are by definition comprised of very few members, it was a very good experience because even the rookies had to carry their weight. This, combined with the ability to talk to the planners and programmers directly, made it a very good and rewarding environment."

For the last two months of the training period, new employees had to pair up in artist-engineer teams to create minigames. "It was a really good opportunity to make a game with an engineer, even if it was a very small game," he said.

Together, Takahashi and the engineer created *Midnight Justice*, a game about bank robbers fleeing from a giant police robot. The player, as a pair of bank robbers, drives and dodges obstacles in the road by changing lanes while also leaning through the sunroof to fire missiles at the robot.

"The biggest point of that game was the camera and game view," Takahashi said. "I wanted to show a police robot that chases you from behind. So, the car the bank robbers are driving and the police robot are facing and coming toward the camera, like one of the levels of *Crash Bandicoot*."

"I think it wasn't bad," he added. "Dodging obstacles and shooting simultaneously was a bit hard though."

When his training period ended, Takahashi's career at Namco continued to evolve.

"Almost all new employees were assigned to actual game projects, besides me," he said. "I was assigned to a small prototype project, because my boss who helped me from my failed interview understood and agreed with my perspective about projects that Namco had at that time. I had no interest in joining a sequel, racing game, gun-shooting game, or fighting game project."

He added, "My boss wanted me to think of a new game idea, but if I joined a big project, it would take a long time to finish. So he picked a small prototype project for me, so I could think about the new game while working. Also, such a small project was a good opportunity to work with some veterans, and I learned a lot."

Takahashi was assigned to work on a new arcade project under development, a unit that functioned as a mix between a public email terminal and a photo booth.

"The funny thing was that they were trying to make a new kiosk that has email and camera functions with cute characters," he said. "You could compose email and attach photos, and of course read emails too. You know, the smartphone hadn't been invented at the time. So I designed that character and some funny decorative stickers and background images, like a *purikura*.[1] But unfortunately, that project was cancelled."

---

1 *Purikura* is the name for *purinto kurabu* or "print club" photo booth/sticker-printing machines. Users step into a booth and pose for photos, before adding stamps, clip art, backgrounds, or other cute decorative features. These images are then printed onto small stickers, which the customers can share with their friends. In the late 90s, Japanese teens often carried small photo albums to collect the 1" x ½" stickers.

Takahashi returned to creative collaboration within his team, trying to come up with concepts that seemed fun but were also different from anything Namco was making. But in the meantime, he had to find another small project to work on.

"In 2000, I moved to a new prototype project called *Action Drive*, a kind of copy of *Crazy Taxi*, but the designer wanted it to be more like a spy game," he said. "I joined as a visual artist and did modeling on a car, a shopping mall, et cetera. The senior artist, who was my boss on that project, and I thought the idea wasn't fun, so we tried to come up with new proposals and pitch the good ones."

It was in this brainstorming session that Takahashi came up with early ideas for a Prince and a King of the Cosmos.

"My idea was, the Queen of the Cosmos was kidnapped by some bad guys on Earth," he said. "The King of the Cosmos wants to help her, but he's lazy, so he lets his son go help her. The obvious problem is that the Prince is smaller than human beings. So he has to use his hammer-shaped head to hit the heads of people driving by, and then hack that human by sticking a small steering wheel on top of their heads while they are stunned. That's one of the reasons why [the characters in *Katamari*] have such wide heads."

Takahashi saw opportunities for new and different types of gameplay within that framework that still fulfilled the designer's original idea.

"I thought that would be kind of a good excuse to do crazy driving, because you're not human, you're the Prince. The King of the Cosmos would give him objectives sometimes, like, 'I think your Mom will be around here, or there, or over there?' He would try to provide correct info for his son, but almost all of it would be wrong. So the Prince had to drive all around the city following these wrong leads."

Unfortunately (or perhaps fortunately for *Katamari* fans), that game designer didn't like the proposed concept. He told Takahashi, "You can use [these characters] for another game."

Soon after, *Action Drive* was cancelled, and Takahashi needed to find a new project. He also found himself evaluating his career at Namco.

"Other artists who joined Namco with me that same year had been on commercial projects that weren't cancelled, or were already released," he said. "I think it was only me who hadn't completed any actual game development at that time. So my boss and I had to choose [what I would do next]: Join a guaranteed-release game project that's not fun, keep looking for a new prototype project, or make my own game."

Like the questions he had raised during his art cram school days about what sort of art he would make when he was on his own, Takahashi knew that there would be challenges associated with going it on his own, but also that path was likely to be the only one that would allow him to create the kind of fun, playful art that might truly make people happier.

KATAMARI
TAKES SHAPE

There's something missing...
Ah-hah! Yes, that's it!
We get it now! It has no mystery.

—The King of All Cosmos

SOMETIMES, OUR BEST IDEAS COME from seeds that were planted much, much earlier. They grow quietly. We spend our time nurturing and feeding them, hoping they get just the right amount of water and sunlight. Many never sprout. But maybe, finally, one day we notice their small, green shoots poking up through the dirt. We don't know what the small green thing is going to look like when it's fully grown, because it will be the product of everything that has gone into the planting: the dirt, the fertilizer, the minerals in the water. But we know that it's on its way to being something beautiful.

Many creative people call this concept "drawing from the well," a term which refers to the collection of inspirations we feed ourselves with, which appear later in our work. Everything that goes into the well comes out again in another form when the "water" is drawn out in the form of a creative idea.

Likewise, in his book *On Writing: A Memoir of the Craft,* Stephen King refers to his story concepts as "fossils," fully-formed ideas that exist in their entirety in his subconscious, which he must endeavor to uncover slowly, with the care of an archaeologist at work on a dig site.

The idea for *Katamari Damacy*, the world it's set in, and its driving principles, emerged for Takahashi in a similar way.

"I got the initial idea for *Katamari* when I was walking back to the station from the office," Takahashi said. "It was nighttime. I had been thinking of and looking for the idea for a game since I joined Namco. I didn't have a particular time set aside to think about games, but my game idea sensor was always on, turning 24 hours a day. And yeah, that sensor is still turning right now."

Takahashi wasn't interested in repeating ideas, or treading familiar ground.

"I was, and am, looking for the ideas that only video games can do, and only I can do—and something new," he said. "Of course, I might be able to think about a fantastic soccer game, or a new car racing game, or an ambitious shooter, but other developers have made those. Also I wanted to make a game that makes people smile, like [the sculptures] I had done at university. So, finding a nice game idea is hard for me, even now."

Takahashi found inspiration in other games that challenged these norms.

At a press conference in 1999, Sony Computer Entertainment showed footage of a game called *Densen*, which translates to "power line." In the video, clusters of four or five Japanese houses float on small islands, suspended in a blue sky, surrounded by puffy white clouds. The sidewalks of these neighborhoods end abruptly, and the islands are connected only by colorful, curling wires.

The player character is a young girl who runs through the streets holding a metal coat hanger, which she uses to hook onto the wires, gliding between the islands and hopping between parallel lines in the air. She spins and flips around, rushing along the lines using power boosts, her hair streaming behind her in the wind.

"That game looked interesting to me," Takahashi said. "The details of gameplay were unclear, but the footage of a player sliding along power lines in the town was so cool and charming to me, because I realized that this ordinary world could be changed to an extraordinarily wonderful world by a very small idea.

Very sadly, this game was not released after all, but it gave me inspiration."

Takahashi also noted in his interview at IndieCade how *Densen* inspired the idea of basing a game on day-to-day life with only a small twist, and how it showed him that a game didn't necessitate combat to be fun. "Fantasy and violence aren't needed to make a great game," he said. "That made me realize that I was wrong in how I was approaching games altogether."

Another source of inspiration Takahashi cited was a game that appears in sports days at Japanese elementary school. Sports days, called *undōkai,* are days set aside for students to compete in large teams and showcase their skills for their friends, parents, and extended family members. Kids work together and practice for weeks ahead of the event, determined to help their team win. It also serves as an important demonstration of strength through unity.

One such game is *tamakorogashi,* in which participants try to push a massive, colored ball into a goal, sometimes while tied together, or after passing it over-head along a line of hundreds of students. An image of school children playing *tamakorogashi* appeared as the cover for the *Katamari Damacy* demo when it eventually debuted at the Tokyo Game Show in 2003.

These concepts churned inside Takahashi, until, as often is the case, inspiration struck suddenly, presenting him with the seed of what would eventually grow into a fully-developed game.

"While walking, I just got inspiration about something spinning very fast, and I thought it would look interesting," Takahashi told me. "After I got on the train, I kept thinking about that spinning stuff. And that spinning stuff had started rolling in my imaginary world, and colliding into other stuff and rolling it up, then getting bigger itself. I think I had a very basic game idea before I got off the train."

"The next night, I had a dinner with my friend who worked as a game designer at Namco, and talked about my idea," he said. "I had talked to him and asked him about game ideas before, because I was not a designer, so I wanted to get advice from an actual game designer. What he said [this time] was, 'Wow, Keita, this is a game!' I had asked him about tons of silly ideas before, so I felt like I made it, finally."

Now that the ball was rolling, it was time to take the concept to Namco.

"The next day, I talked to my boss about my idea, and he understood it immediately," Takahashi said. "I suggested we use the characters I designed for the *Action Drive* project, the Prince and King of the Cosmos. The Prince is small so you can start this game from a very small level and get to a big one, and the King of the Cosmos is just crazy. It was a perfect match. And my boss said, 'Good job Takahashi-kun, you made it finally.' I know it was just an idea and not actually a game yet, but we were on the same page already."

So how does someone take an idea for a game from concept to reality? It's easier said than done, especially in the hierarchical structure of a Japanese video game company.

•

Japanese business culture relies deeply on tradition and relationships, including loyalty to one's team, boss, and the company itself. In many companies, employees who join directly after graduating can expect to retire from that same company 40 years later, although a study on video game developers in Japan revealed the average time spent in the game industry is closer to six or seven years.

Internally, Japanese company structures and customs are often highly regimented. The long-term relationship that an employee develops with a company also leads to strong bonds between managers and their employees, and among teammates. Although their in-office interactions can appear formal and are often based on a "master-apprentice" model, this rigidity exists to achieve collective harmony: Everyone knows what to expect.

As long as employees grow their networks, avoid mistakes, and don't rock the boat, their career growth over time is fairly predictable. This is especially important in a society where everything from romantic relationships to housing applications to a child's grade school acceptance can be affected by one's job and the corresponding status it affords them.

However, sometimes that requirement of loyalty results in tough times and unhealthy lifestyles for employees, including long workday hours simply for the sake of appearance or because a boss is still present on site. Game developers in particular experience long periods of what's known as "crunch," in which teams work intensely for extended hours and on weekends in order to finish a product by a deadline—sometimes for months at a time, and at the cost of time spent on family, sleep, and general well-being.

Takahashi's path through Namco was ordinary in some ways. For example, his departmental shuffling to find the best fit is a fairly standard practice for new employees at Japanese companies. Atypical, though, was his ambition to create a new kind of game, and his willingness to speak up and fight for his point of view rather than conform to the wishes of his superiors.

This is most evident in the fact that no clearly laid-out internal process within Namco existed to pitch a game design from the position Takahashi held or the department he was in.

"I talked with [Mitsutoshi] Ozaki-san, my boss, about how we should move this idea forward to an actual internal production," Takahashi said. "Usually game ideas were proposed from the game design department at Namco, but we both worked in the art department. Also, technically Ozaki-san was not my actual boss at that time. He had moved to another department, so I had to talk to my current boss about my idea first—but he was not a manager of game designers, he was a manager of artists. He seemed to not have a bad impression of my idea, but he couldn't make a decision about the game itself."

Faced with that institutional obstacle, there seemed to be no clear path forward, but Takahashi pushed on anyway.

"It sucked, and I was stuck," Takahashi said. "But Ozaki-san had suggested a very unusual method for moving forward to me. At that time, I think he worked in the 'new business department' where they explore new business models. And that department was going to establish a specialized school for making video games for Namco by collaborating with a school for learning computer graphics called Digital Hollywood."

The Namco Digital Hollywood Game Lab was a six-month course designed to help developers learn skills necessary for creating games for the PlayStation 2. Instructors were selected from Namco's development staff, and included people who had worked on titles such as *Soulcalibur* and *Tekken*.

Like the Konami education program that had produced *Beatmania*, *Dance Dance Revolution*, and *GuitarFreaks*, Namco's hope was that their program would produce new and interesting work while funneling graduates into new hires, resulting in a reduction in the in-house training usually required of new recruits.

"Ozaki-san said that Masaya Nakamura, then president of Namco, was interested in being a school principal, and that is one of the big reasons for this business," Takahashi said. "And this game class had a curriculum where they actually make a game. But the students of this school [were] learn[ing] to be CG artists. So Ozaki-san needed a game idea that was easy to collaborate on with very junior artists, and my idea was selected. Ozaki-san thought the students could make objects that a katamari can roll up."

The plan for the class was to produce a prototype game, and if that went well, to create a fully-fleshed out product.

Takahashi recognized that this was a high-risk project. "But I felt that it was so much better than joining boring other projects," Takahashi said. "So I decided to join this project as game designer."

Work on the prototype for *Katamari Damacy* went forward as planned, with Digital Hollywood staff members and contributors pulled from wherever the team could get them.

"The students of Digital Hollywood worked on the modeling," Takahashi said. "Fortunately, we [got] a lead visual designer from Namco, but we had to find engineers who could work with us. Almost all departments at Namco declined to provide their engineers to us because our project was very unclear and they were very busy developing their games. And then it turned out that a department that makes arcade games was going to lay off some mechanical engineers, and it sounded like some of them had coding experience. So we asked them: *Get fired or code our project?* And then they chose to work with us."

The prototype came together quickly, encouraged by upcoming deadlines and technological constraints. The team was made up of Takahashi, three Namco programmers, three visual designers, and ten to twelve vocational college students.

The development of the prototype was speedy, lasting less than six months.

"One of the goals was to exhibit a *Katamari* prototype at Japan Media Arts Festival," Takahashi said. "Of course, the biggest goal was to make this project into an actual commercial product."

Picking the right development platform was the next challenge for the small team.

At that time in the early 2000s, Sony, Sega, Nintendo, and Microsoft were all deep underway in developing the next generation of consoles. The industry was transitioning from 2D computer graphics to 3D, which included better texture mapping, lighting, and shading; shifting from chunky ROM cartridges to CD-ROM discs; and introducing overall better audio, video, color, and resolution.

The PlayStation, which used discs, dominated the scene, having become the first home console to sell 100 million units globally. Its rival Nintendo 64, which had stuck to the cartridge format and suffered delays in its initial release, held a distant second place at close to 33 million lifetime sales, boasting a number of popular first party titles but failing to attract as many third party developers.

The Nintendo 64 had nevertheless "truly brought developers into the era of 3D," said Nintendo president Shigeru Miyamoto in a 2000 interview. The technology of the N64 allowed them to work in "real 3D" as opposed to the "pseudo-3D" of the PlayStation, in which developers had to write their own code to bring 3D objects to the screen and didn't have the ability to easily display textures in the correct perspective.

However, it had been tough for game-makers to develop for the Nintendo 64 because of difficulties with using its hardware and delays in Nintendo's release of development software libraries.

With this in mind, the next Nintendo console, the GameCube, was designed from the beginning to be developer-friendly, with new architecture and a more powerful system. "We thought about the developers as our main customers," said GameCube chip developer ArtX's Greg Buchner in a 2001 interview with the Gaming Intelligence Agency.

As the GameCube was being developed, Sony was working on the PlayStation 2 (PS2). They released specs for the console, which introduced its new CPU (central processing unit), the "Emotion Engine."

As with all consoles at the time, the PS2 CPU was designed for a specific task—in this case running 3D games—as opposed to consoles today, which use operating systems and perform a variety of tasks, and must therefore be more flexible in their processing capabilities.

But the PS2 documentation and development libraries were outdated, and Sony didn't provide a development kit or software tools to make the process of creating games easier for potential developers. Instead the company assumed that the developer would just figure out the new hardware, perhaps hoping that the resulting games would be better for having overcome the struggle. Although it's since gone down in history as the best-selling console of all time, the PS2 maintained a reputation of being extremely difficult to develop for.

Between Nintendo's developer-friendly outreach and the released specs for the PS2 indicating it would be a difficult path for even experienced game developers, the choice was clear to the *Katamari* team: Even though they wanted to release the game on the PS2, they needed to use the GameCube platform to develop the prototype.

"Our engineer didn't have much expertise, and neither did I, and the schedule was tight," Takahashi said. "So for these reasons we picked the Nintendo GameCube platform for prototyping. I wanted to use the PS2 controller though."

Once the game prototype was in progress and the choice of development console locked down, the team needed to figure out how to actually make the game, given their relative lack of experience.

"I had been working as director of this prototyped project even though I didn't have any experience as a designer or director," Takahashi said. "Of course Ozaki-san helped me a lot, but basically he trusted me." Ozaki believed in Takahashi's vision enough that he signed on to personally work on the game as a UI Artist.

Takahashi's role as director stretched his imagination and forced him to develop new skill sets.

"This is a very obvious thing, but I had to think up everything about the game," he said. "The music was one of the [more] important things, and we had tried to make a music system that interacts with the size of the katamari for this prototype. That means, the music gets richer as the katamari is getting bigger—and we actually made it. But it felt like there were many restrictions to making an interactive music system, and it made the composing very hard."

Takahashi identified two problems with the interactive music system. First, the music was very basic at the start of the game, which makes it noticeable when it becomes more complex as the katamari grows. But once the tunes hit a certain level of saturation, it was difficult to recognize differences in the music. Second, a technical issue prevented the implementation some of Takahashi's original game design ideas, which also affected the music.

Part of *Katamari*'s gameplay involves ramming the katamari into objects or parts of the environment, which can sometimes knock pieces off of the current ball, reducing its overall size. "I hoped making the katamari [shrink] by failing would also be kinda fun," Takahashi said. In his original plan, as the katamari got smaller, the music would also return to its more simple form.

According to a 2015 interview with the entertainment website Games Radar, Takahashi wanted hundreds of items in each of the gameplay areas, which "meant each object had to have the lowest possible polygon count so as to not overload PS2's limited system memory. The team looked for things that were simple in shape and that had some heft to them, but that wouldn't look awful without anti-aliasing." But even at these low polygon counts, the memory capacity of the PS2 simply wasn't large enough to store every single item that the katamari had rolled up since the start of the level, making it impossible to shrink the katamari beyond a certain size.

This technical problem would turn out to be an unexpected boon to the quality of the gameplay. "Almost all the players didn't feel that [becoming] small again was fun," Takahashi said. "That meant the music would just be rich and gorgeous intentionally, and we wouldn't make it interactive. So we changed the plan of music from this interactive idea to [the now-]familiar music direction."

The team completed the prototype, and Takahashi reported that internal satisfaction with the product was high. Excitement over the project continued to grow.

"The students of Digital Hollywood were happy with what they made, and we exhibited [the prototype] at the Japan Media Arts Festival," he said. "I think it went very well. And we did a presentation internally. Many employees of Namco came and played *Katamari*, and they liked it. Also Ozaki-san had some meetings with executives."

The prototype had done its job. *Katamari Damacy* would become a larger game, to be released by Namco for the PlayStation 2.

•

The meetings between Ozaki and the executives went well. "The deal was, I got a budget to develop *Katamari* for PS2—yeah!—but I had to work with an external development company—nooo!" Takahashi said.

The studio Now Production was selected to help navigate the difficult architecture of the PlayStation 2. Takahashi was worried that working with a larger team could compromise his vision for *Katamari*. Also, Now Production was based in Osaka, which is two hours away from Tokyo by bullet train.

But any initial concerns were quickly resolved when the teams began working together and found a good rapport. "I had very mixed feelings [about the arrangement at first], but fortunately I got a small, talented artist team, who were capable of doing art direction with an external company," Takahashi said.

There were around twenty people on the team, with half in Tokyo, and half in Osaka.

Production on the full version of *Katamari Damacy* began in late 2001, with a budget of around ¥100 million, equivalent to between $650,000 and $800,000 USD at the time, or $1.1 million as of this writing.

"The lead programmer [Kazumi Yamabe] and the lead designer [Masatoshi Ogita] were from Now Production, and the [object and map] designer [Minori Kubota] was in Tokyo at Namco," Takahashi said in an interview with Edge Online. "Around 90 percent of the work was done in Osaka. I was nervous—it was my first time as director on a game—but I could visualize what I was aiming for, so it was just a matter of working towards it."

Directing *Katamari Damacy* meant spending time at both locations and overseeing both teams.

"Usually I worked at that external company, then came back to Tokyo once every three weeks," he said. "I'd stay in Tokyo a week, then back to Osaka. That was my life around the beginning of the 21st century."

After development began, the team stayed busy, but it was a smooth and drama-free process without any major obstacles.

Takahashi said that he learned a lot about managing teams, and how effective communication is essential in creating the best possible game.

"In making *Katamari* I learned that at a game studio, we don't need partitions or instant messengers," he said. "The most important thing is to talk directly to each other as a team. By doing so we were able to develop a game exactly as we wanted. I think that really shows." However, he also discovered that there is a time for collaboration and a time for sticking to one's own singular vision.

"I worked on the basic concept on my own," he said, in a December 2004 postmortem with *Game Developer Magazine*. "I found that if I started to listen to others, the concept tended to become diluted and unfocused.

However, once the basic concept was decided, it was helpful to have open discussions with the team. There were many more ideas that were not used in the game, but I still got something out of all the different ideas that were brought up—even if I didn't use them as they were presented."

THE SUM OF ITS PARTS

Oh?? What a nice katamari.
Substantial, yet goes down smooth.

—The King of All Cosmos

WHENEVER YOU COMPLETE A LEVEL in *Katamari Damacy*, the King's head appears with a cymbal crash, returning to the world in order to collect the Prince and the now-full, sparkling katamari and convey them both back to the cosmos. The new katamari is converted into a star via his Royal Rainbow, a multi-colored pathway that spews out of his mouth and collects his passengers.

This general structure forms the basis for all other levels in the game: Roll, grow, and deliver your new star to dad. Once you've played *Katamari* for a few minutes, you know how to play the rest of the game. So exploring the ways that the levels vary—in complexity, difficulty, location, design and layout, time limit, and tone—is where much of the joy of the game lies.

Each of *Katamari*'s 22 levels has four objectives. First, the King gives you an assignment, either to create a star of a certain size, or to collect a specific number or type of object in order to create a constellation. The second objective is to beat the level's timer. These are the only two tasks required to complete a level and open the next one.

An optional third objective is to collect Royal Presents, gift boxes hidden in difficult-to-reach places, which contain equippable decorative objects like hats and masks. And the fourth is to locate and roll up a Cousin on each level, a tiny figure with a funny-shaped head kinda like yours, who will become a playable character later on.

Whether it's the King's silly starting dialogue, a new catchy tune on the soundtrack, a katamari with a pretty new design, or even just the way a row of bananas is arranged to lure you down a road, each level feels like a new and interesting variation on the game's core design.

The world of the game becomes a bit more fantastical as the game proceeds. Sometimes you encounter everyday animals that, according to your in-game catalog, have human names. Sometimes you see funny tableaus such as students out for school picture day. Occasionally you'll find things that are downright strange, like a child's chalk graffiti that lifts off the ground to contribute to your overall size, or characters like Momotaro, a boy from Japanese mythology who was born inside a giant peach.

These whimsical touches are part of why game designer Robin Hunicke believes the game is revolutionary: "[T]hat is not something that we celebrate when we're adults, in this culture: the kind of childlike wonder that you feel."

Nothing ever feels like it was added for the sake of sheer randomness. The objects may be mythological in origin, or comically oversized, but there's an inherent logic to their placement, a sense of physicality mirroring the way objects feel and behave in real life, that binds this world together.

To Hunicke, it's this coherence that is the game's greatest achievement. "[*Katamari*] is a seamless collaboration between level design, physical movement, narrative, and visual design," she told me. "Everything that you pick up in the game is important to how you move. And then also everything you pick up creates this feedback system that influences where you can go, so it's completely tied together."

But for Takahashi and his team, creating *Katamari*'s seamlessness was far from easy.

•

The concept of *Katamari Damacy* is, at its heart, a simple one: Roll a ball around and collect items. But getting that gameplay exactly right, and figuring out what would be the most fun for players, became the main goals that consumed the team during the game's development.

"As a home entertainment game, would it be okay if you just roll?" Takahashi recalled asking, speaking at his GDC postmortem session. "Other people raise the question about my game: They said we should put in more interesting features. The company and other game designers criticized me, but I really enjoyed rolling the katamari by using the two sticks. Therefore, I proactively ignored the suggestions."

Continuing in the *Game Developer Magazine* postmortem, Takahashi outlined the reason he had adhered so strictly to simplicity, given the climate of games at the time of *Katamari*'s creation.

"It's great that there are many types of video games, but I've always wanted to create something different that can only be done in a game," he said. "If you are going to play a game that resembles a movie, you should just watch a movie. And if you are going to play a game that shows realistic cars, wouldn't it be more fun to drive a real car?"

"Of course, I do understand the fun aspects of these games," he added. "Moving freely in beautifully drawn environments or driving a car you'll never be able to own—those are definitely fun experiences. But lately, there are just too many of those types of games. And I think it has become boring. Games these days are also really complicated. There are lots of buttons and there are lots of items to keep track of. I'm just tired of all those complications. To hold a controller in your hand and control the action displayed on the screen is a minor thing nowadays, but I still think it's a little miracle. There's no need to add a lot of extra stuff to make it more difficult."

In his 2005 GDC talk, Takahashi elaborated: By advocating for simplicity, he sought to change in how people experienced games.

"Although I said I would like to make a game which is easily understood by everyone, I do not mean simple is best," he said through a translator. "I don't think something easily understood is necessarily simple."

To Takahashi, removing the clutter of the interaction and interface meant that you could make room for truer human experiences and more nuanced expressions of feelings. He gave the example of complex human relationships with many ups and downs. "You might sweat, sometimes you stop talking to anybody, or you get angry at something." And yet those complex relationships could still be boiled down to a single word: "'love,' or 'those teenage years.'"

That's the simplicity that Takahashi strives for. A game should not "try to incorporate a lot of elements so that the game itself looks very complicated," but should instead achieve "that point where you can express complicated situations by one word."

"The simple method is, for example," Takahashi said, "rolling the ball, absorbing, making the ball, making the ball as big as possible." Simple concepts that can make a big impact for players.

•

Just like a katamari, the game's scale is constantly adjusting, growing larger and larger as the player progresses. Each level's challenges shift just enough each time to keep the player always wanting to move forward, whether it's the addition of more time or the challenge to avoid a particular type of object until the katamari has grown to a particular size.

The sizes of levels also grow as the katamari size goals increase, beginning in various rooms of the house, eventually expanding to include other rooms of the house and the garden area beyond, then the street beyond, then the entirety of Pigeon Town, and eventually the surrounding city, continent, and globe. The speed with which the katamari attains these goals adjusts proportionately, so the player always feels a sense of steady growth.

Upon reaching the size goal, at which point the current size of the katamari is compared to a game object (for example, a katamari of 21 cm 8 mm is as big as 3,455 in-game mahjong game tiles), the player can choose to either exit the level or continue it until the time runs out.

Players also get a sense of what it's like to grow a katamari. Collecting the larger objects in the garden allows the player to return to the living room again, where a new set of objects, including things which had previously been walls or obstacles, are now available for absorption: paperback novels, cassette tapes, an *omurice* (omelette rice dish).

In his essay "The Prince of Objects: Katamari and Ontology," game developer and internet artist Darius Kazemi discusses the way the player experiences this adjustment:

> For myself, *Katamari's* primary delight came from the slow realization that things which appeared to be static when the Prince's ball is small turn out to be dynamic when the scale changes. You might spend the first five minutes of a level rolling around a house. The house is immovable and non-interactive, comprising of a maze for you to traverse and collect the smaller items that it make their home within its walls. But five minutes later

you're 50 meters in diameter and can pick up the entire house as easily as if it were a ballpoint pen!

For another example of *Katamari*'s use of scale, Kazemi looks at the game's public park levels.

> At the small scale, you find yourself inside the park, working your way up from popsicles to picnic baskets to punk rockers. But at a certain scale, those objects become abstracted into the notion of a "park" as an object on its own. You can no longer pick up a single popsicle—you're too big. This is related to a concept in game engines called "level of detail" or "LOD". [...] Yes, we can and do appreciate the individual elements of a park, but at some level we close that box and begin to refer to the park as an object in and of itself. What was inside the park no longer exists, and is subsumed by the "park" object.

This design choice was of course largely dictated by the memory limitations of the PlayStation 2 system. If *Katamari* were made today, it would likely feel different, since consoles now have enough memory to store that list of every item the katamari had rolled up. Takahashi's original vision of being able to reduce the ball from its biggest size to its smallest would be possible to implement, rather than necessitating the workarounds that resulted in the version of the game we know.

But that adherence to that sense of scale and reality is also an important part of Takahashi's work, and a theme that he's explored from his time studying sculpture in school, to now.

"There's a physicality to Keita's designs," Ricky Haggett told me in an interview. Haggett is the designer of the games *Hohokum* and *Loot Rascals*, as well as *Tenya Wanya Teens*, a collaboration with Takahashi that blends a digital game and a physical controller with sixteen glowing buttons, like a small arcade cabinet. "It's not just a whimsical silly thing that would only work in a video game because you have computers. His games have a solidity to them. The fun is in that they feel like how things would feel in the real world if you were really playing with a real thing."

"You can't imagine Keita making an ethereal, floaty, non-physics-y thing," Haggett added. "The stuff he makes has a solidity and a tactile, lumpy physicality about it that is part of that same process of how he came up with it." The same could be said about Takahashi's work going all the way back to the sculptures he made as a student.

The world of *Katamari Damacy* is full of objects, ranging from among the smallest, such as the 2 cm 2 mm mosquito, to some of the largest, like the 240-meter giant octopus, a creature larger than many of the game's small islands.

Each object rolled up by the player is added to an in-game encyclopedia that records everything found, which adds an additional dimension to gameplay if players wish to replay levels to hunt for specific objects to complete their collections.

This vast collection serves another purpose, too. By filling the world with familiar objects, the player is able to quickly assess the size of their katamari in relation to the items around it. As the katamari grows in scale, its movement becomes more laborious and lumbering. The change is visceral and tactile, communicating everything the player needs to intuitively understand how much strength they have gained.

In its way, *Pac-Man* is a sort of precursor to *Katamari Damacy*, with a round object gobbling up everything in its path. Perhaps proud of that connection, Namco has released a Katamari/Pac-Man crossover—in a Pac-Man-themed bonus level that appeared in 2011's *Katamari Amore* and 2012's *Katamari Damacy Mobile 2*. Several Katamari sequels also contain *Pac-Man* Easter eggs such as arcade cabinets and the character of Mac, a video game-loving Royal Cousin who displays Pac-Man images on her face.

In his 2004 interview with GameSpy, *Pac-Man* creator Toru Iwatani described *Katamari Damacy* as a new branch of innovative gaming, "an entirely new concept" that the company was very proud of.

"Namco, as a company, has built itself on games like that, games with new concepts," Iwatani said. "Namco, the company that created one of the few no-button best-sellers (*Pac-Man*) is looking for simplicity and innovation, a new genre that the company describes as 'romantic adventure.'"

However, as much as both *Pac-Man* and *Katamari Damacy* are about clearing space, progression in *Pac-Man* means faster and stronger enemies while its gameplay, and its player character, remain largely the same.

In *Katamari*, it's the changing scale, and the increasing speed at which larger sizes can be reached, that distinguishes play on later levels. The actions the player is taking are the same, but they, along with their katamari, have grown in power.

KATAMARI ON A ROLL

But now that you've come this far,
We would love to have a much bigger, super-nice
katamari.

—The King of All Cosmos

KATAMARI DAMACY DEBUTED at the Tokyo Game Show in September 2003 with a one-level demo.

One writer in attendance, GameSpot's Jeff Gerstmann, called *Katamari* "one of those games that defy classification," praising its "cool visual style" and "good dose of weird fun."

Takahashi was too busy working on the game to attend the show, but he was relieved to hear that the feedback was positive. "I [realized] what I wanted to make was not wrong after all," Takahashi told me.

"It was very lucky, because Sony really liked *Katamari*, and they wanted us to release it a little bit earlier than we planned, since they wanted good numbers for that fiscal term," Takahashi said. "So the early due date was hard, but they helped us with advertising on TV and elsewhere."

In March, 2004, IGN described *Katamari*'s advertising presence on the streets of Japan, noting how they had "spotted billboards and poster ads for the game all over the city, with many stores even carrying demo units" in the weeks leading up to the game's release.

"Actually, what they made for TV was a million times better than Namco's ad," Takahashi added, laughing.

One fifteen-second ad features a man waiting for an appointment. A secretary welcomes him, but instead of rising to meet her, he rolls forward, attached to the couch he's been sitting on. The couch rolls forward and sticks to the secretary. The mass then rolls to the elevator and enters it, picking up more furniture, a janitor, and finally, the boss.

Even the cover art for *Katamari Damacy* was notably different. Takahashi wasn't a fan of covers that are "game industry oriented," with designs that feature the main characters, preferring a cover that demonstrates something about what you can expect from the gameplay.

The cover art depicts a beautiful blue sky over a grassy field, complete with a perfect rainbow, beautiful flowers, and grazing cows. Mt. Fuji, the highest mountain in Japan, is visible in the distance, small behind a cityscape, which itself is in the midst of being rolled up by a giant, object-laden katamari that looms over them both.

"I just wanted to make a cover that was good," he said about the final design. "That cover means: Big."

Katamari Damacy was released on March 18, 2004. It sold 35,083 units during its first week, making it the top-selling game in Japan. It was priced at about 4,000 yen, about two-thirds of the usual price of a new game at the time.

Game companies in Japan typically determine a game's success by its sales in the first two to three weeks in stores, so strong sales during that time are usually crucial to a game's future potential, including the development of sequels. According to IGN, Namco originally estimated that over 500,000 units would be sold in Japan in its first year, an optimistic figure for a first-time property.

But *Katamari Damacy*'s sales and orders from retailers remained steady week-to-week, and it remained in the top ten games sold for nine weeks, when it was finally bumped down to number nineteen with the re-release of the Classic NES Series (known in Japan as the Famicom Mini Series) for Game Boy Advance. By the end of this tenth week, *Katamari* had sold a respectable 102,976 copies.

"I think sales were not as good as we, and they, had expected," Takahashi said. "But it was good for a new IP [intellectual property]. I hope Namco could recoup the all money they spent to develop the game, at least."

The sales numbers were apparently satisfactory enough to order a sequel, which was announced in December that year, slated for release in spring 2005. But it turns out it wasn't only the sales numbers that helped in the decision to support further development of *Katamari Damacy* games. Toru Iwatani, Head of Namco Research and Development, believed it was *Katamari Damacy*'s uniqueness—and even its small scale—that made it especially appealing to the company.

"I think there are going to be a lot more genres opening up, and I see video games branching out more in the future," Iwatani told GameSpy in 2004. "[*Katamari Damacy*] is one example of the kinds of games that I am referring to. It is an entirely new concept. Namco, as a company, has built itself on games like that, games with new concepts."

He identified some of Namco's popular titles, like *Soulcalibur* and *Tekken*, which regularly take "$10 million to create," and compared them to *Katamari Damacy*, which was developed for "approximately one-tenth of what he would expect to spend on the bigger titles."

"You also see a trend with games becoming more and more complicated," Iwatani added. "It's difficult for the casual gamer to pick these up and enjoy them. Namco has been trying to put forth simpler games… games that are much more intuitive." It is perhaps no surprise that the creator of *Pac-Man*, a game that uses only a joystick and no buttons, would appreciate this aspect of *Katamari Damacy*'s design.

But despite Namco's faith in the game, at the time of its Japanese release there were no plans to import *Katamari Damacy* to North America. Would the rest of the world forever miss out on the pleasures of rolling a katamari?

•

Thanks to internet hype, excitement had been growing globally about *Katamari Damacy* since its debut at the Tokyo Game Show in 2003. But America's first view into the colorful world of *Katamari Damacy* came during the Game Developers Conference (GDC) in 2004, in the third year of a session called the Experimental Games Workshop (EGW).

The EGW's stated mission is to seek out and showcase "games that take interesting approaches to interactivity that haven't been tried before," admitting that while the definition is "unavoidably vague," the event welcomes games at any level of completion, as it "favor[s] the process of experimentation over the success of results."

Several months before GDC 2004, one of EGW's founders, Robin Hunicke—at the time, an AI researcher and game designer at Northwestern University as well as a member of the International Game Developers Association (IGDA) education committee—was one of a group of game developers who visited the Tokyo Game Show (TGS), one of the world's largest video game expos, looking for new and unusual games they could showcase.

The previous year, the EGW had featured a demonstration of Masaya Matsuura's rhythm game *Mojib-Ribbon*, a game where the vocal track was generated through speech synthesis and whose watercolor art aesthetics formed a clear visual inspiration for later games like *Okami*. After that success, the colleagues visited the TGS floor looking for something unique to showcase.

They walked around the show floor for most of the day, according to Hunicke, "not really [seeing] anything too spectacular." But Hunicke, who had an interest in obscure Japanese games, had read about a strange "snowball" or "dung beetle" simulator and was determined to try it out.

"At that time, games were really like, 'shoot stuff,' or race, or do sports— there weren't even really music games at that time," Hunicke said. "So I had been reading up about *Katamari* a little bit, seeing this 'dung beetle' game that was gonna be at TGS, and I was like, alright, I can't wait to see it."

After a bit of searching, they located the Namco booth, and in the back corner, found what they were looking for.

"It was this tiny little screen in a wall, with this little shelf controller, and there was some stuff around it in Japanese," Hunicke said. "I picked up the controller, and I was like, *This is the greatest thing that I have ever seen in my life.*"

They spent an hour and a half playing—and knew they had found the game the EGW needed.

Afterwards, Doug Church, technical director at Eidos Interactive and IGDA member, wrote in an email published by Gamasutra:

> [I]t was very simple and very direct. Roll the ball around, pick stuff up, it behaves as expected. There are only a few rules to get in the way of the player just acting as they see fit. It was certainly one of the most natural uses of physics in a game, very unforced. That went well with its visual style and overall presentation. Little touches like dogs (stuck in a ball of dung) still moving their legs and such. From the quick view we got at TGS, it was just a very coherent-seeming product, very nicely structured.

The first two years of the EGW had been largely focused on showcasing games created during an associated event, the Indie Game Jam, as well as newly-designed, as-yet-unreleased peripherals such as the guitar controller for *Guitar Hero* from Harmonix. People loved the session and the games it was cheerleading: In a sea of huge studio sequels, these works created by a small, talented, group of independent developers felt fresh and exciting.

"[Asking Namco] if it would be alright if we could have Takahashi-san come over and show the game [was] a big deal, because at that time, Japanese game developers didn't really come to [US industry-centric] GDC very often," Hunicke said. "They certainly didn't talk about experimental gameplay or their process. The talks that we had in the past from Japanese developers at GDC had been [like], after the game comes out, they would show you a bunch of beautiful art and talk about how amazing the game is, but they weren't really that deep on design. And we were trying to change that."

By the time the third year of the EGW came around, the word of mouth about the novelty of the session paid off: On the day of the panel in March 2004, the room was filled to the brim, with people lining the walls and sitting in the aisles.

Onstage, Takahashi stretched his arms as he was introduced. He wore a t-shirt emblazoned with bold, block letters: ROCK AND ROLL. A tiny pink cocktail umbrella sat on the lectern in front of him. Colorful, animated, hand-illustrated letters filled the screen behind him as he explained how the game worked.

"The person in green is a hero," he explained through a translator. "His height is only five centimeters."

He used only four slides in the demonstration, each with a single animated word to describe the actions of the game. "Rotate." "Absorb." Then 100 tiny copies of word "big" filling the background of the slide with an illustration of a small ball growing into a large one, and a picture of the game's cover art.

The only appreciable difference between this version of the cover and the final artwork is that, in the EGW version, Mt. Fuji is spewing a huge black cloud. In the final piece, the sky is clear.

Then, Takahashi offered a demonstration of the game in action. As the game's start screen appeared, the casually-sung words of the now-iconic theme song filled the room: "*Nah… nah nah nah nah nah nah nah.*"

"I'm from Namco," Takahashi said. "So first of all, I'd like to absorb the name 'Namco' to begin this game." The crowd chuckled appreciatively as he pushed both joysticks forward and the Prince rolled the ball toward the logo, picking up the letters "NA," delighting the audience with a demonstration of the gameplay in an unexpected place. In a 2011 interview with Kill Screen, Takahashi spoke about the philosophies that guide his design choices:

> When making video games, I've tried to develop them in such a way so they may be enjoyed by anyone. Also, I believe that things other than

what's usually considered the game, such as a settings/options screen, can be a part of play. Gameplay isn't just inside the game—everything is the game. Everything should be part of the fun.

The EGW audience's laughter grew as they watched the game's opening movie, in all its absurd glory and backed by a rollicking tune.

As he played through the first level, Takahashi described the story of the game, telling the audience about the King of All Cosmos and his son, the Prince's adventures. Laughter and spontaneous applause broke out as the katamari grew in size, absorbing socks, vegetables, and animals from the garden. After a few minutes of gameplay, he switched to show a video of the katamari once it has grown to city-size, capable of absorbing people off the street, and then buildings off the continent.

One final gameplay demo showed off the end credits, in which the Prince is rolling a katamari across the globe, picking up each individual country as he goes. "I could say I made this game just for this screen," Takahashi added.

Darius Kazemi was in that audience that day. He wrote that "the feeling in that room when Keita showed *Katamari* was just electric. It was amazing to see all these game developers, literally the best of the best in the world, in complete awe of this weird little game. At the end of the presentation, when he said there were no plans to port it to the US market, everyone was just devastated."

As Takahashi and the fans would soon learn, the excitement generated by that presentation was enough to move mountains.

•

Against the odds, demand for *Katamari Damacy* in the West continued to grow. The game's performance in Japan, the positive reviews from the reviews of Tokyo Game Show, and the excitement generated by the Experimental Game Workshop, meant that the American press was eager to receive the odd game they referred to as "Namco's snowball simulator."

Takahashi later stated that the positivity generated by the EGW led directly to him being invited to participate at the Electronic Entertainment Expo (E3), as well as resulting in the American release.

And the press loved it. When *Katamari Damacy* was released in North America on September 22, 2004 for $20, positive reviews flowed in.

"One of the best games that I've played all year," wrote GameSpy, noting that they wished it was longer. 1UP agreed: "Simply put, this is one of the most original and entertaining games we've come across in ages."

Many outlets spoke specifically to the feelings of joy that it evoked in them. "It's the happiest game I've ever played, and the happiness is infectious," wrote Eurogamer, while IGN stated, "It's something that's fun, something that's happy, and something that's so well put together and so enjoyable, whatever faults it may have fade behind the laughter and smiles it so effortlessly creates."

Reviewers also wrote about the game's aesthetic and music as a major selling point. GameSpot called the game "unapologetically surreal, which can make it tough to look away from," and PSX Extreme praised the game's "surreal *Yellow Submarine* style cinemas, the happy-happy music, [and] the twisted dialogue."

Others called attention to *Katamari Damacy's* singular, cohesive vision. *Edge* magazine wrote, "When so many games are trying to defend their value by cramming every mode and style into one unpalatable mix, it's refreshing to play something that's conceived with such vibrant, capricious clarity. "

Reviewers also noted its uniqueness. G4 TV wrote, "*Katamari Damacy* is interactive happiness. Charming, exuberant, and shameless, it's a rare game in today's world of self-aware first-person shooters and freeform crime simulators."

It also turned out to be a treat for people who had played the Japanese-only version, and got to experience the English-language localization by Agness Kaku for the first time upon its American release.

"Clearly, I was already a huge fan of the game," said Robin Hunicke in a January 2005 blog post. "But when the localized version came out—it was an even better experience. Suddenly, the Prince's world was full of humor and depth—and the structure of the game and its missions made sense in a whole new way. How many times do we get that opportunity—to play a game just for its mechanics and dynamics, and then later, experience these things with the story added back in?"

Retailers hadn't anticipated the demand, boosted by the near-universal positive reviews and the low $20 price tag. Many shops sold out of copies within hours of being stocked, leaving potential fans to scour stores in the hopes of finding one.

The game's popularity came as a surprise at a time when most game studios were reluctant to take on new intellectual properties. In the *Chicago Tribune*, Levi Buchanan noted that Microsoft's *Fable* was the only original property among the 50 top-selling games of 2004. Over the next year, *Katamari Damacy*'s popularity continued to grow at a slow but steady rate. By October 2005, it had sold just over 300,000 copies in the US.

Katamari earned multiple awards and accolades. It was included as one of *Time* magazine's "best games of the year," it won "Best Game Design" and "Innovation

Award" at the 2005 Game Developers Choice Awards, and scored a win for "Best Innovation" from G4's G-Phoria awards (at which the host, actor Wilmer Valderrama, arrived onstage attached to a giant, junk-covered katamari).

Katamari also won both the Academy of Interactive Arts and Sciences Interactive Achievement Award for "Outstanding Design" and an IGDA Game Developer's Choice Award for game design.

For much of the rest of the games industry, though, it was business as usual. The prevailing wisdom of the time could be summed up in a quote from Wedbush Morgan Securities analyst Michael Pachter's 2005 interview with *GameSpot*. "The best business for a publisher is to give people what you know they want," Pachter said. "And what you know they want is a sequel to what they wanted last time. So we don't see a whole lot of innovation. […] [F]or the most part there's no money in innovation, even if it's great."

The market, however, begged to differ. The video game industry was reckoning with sales figures indicating a shocking 18% slump in 2005 holiday season sales compared to the previous year. Analysts blamed a lack of originality as a major reason for the decline, with *Katamari Damacy* often cited in discussions about the challenges publishers face in supporting new, innovative material.

In 2005, *Katamari Damacy* was held up as an example of what the video game industry should aspire to, in a "state of the industry" speech at E3 by Douglas Lowenstein, president of the Entertainment Software Association:

> "[One] issue we need to address is creating more complete game experiences. Keita Takahashi, creator of the game *Katamari Damacy* for Namco, [...] said at GDC that games should "be a happy part of life. I want to try to represent the feelings of love or of being young." How many games do you know that do that? And how many more people would play games, of all ages, if they did?

> [W]e need games with more emotional impact. [...] Games already do trigger a myriad of emotional responses including excitement, fear, gratification, success, pride, triumph, and more. But the Holy Grail for game designers should not be making games that do everything movies do. If that is our ultimate aspiration, we cannot lay claim to being the entertainment media of the 21st century.

> [...] We need games with better stories, more interesting and complex characters, games that

keep you up in the middle of the night wrestling with whether you made the right ethical or moral choices, games that stay with you when you're done with them, games that make you happy when you play them—and afterwards."

During one of gaming's biggest creative and financial slumps, it was *Katamari* that pointed the way forward.

KATAMARI NAH-NAH

We have a piano lesson now.

—The King of All Cosmos

KATAMARI'S MUSICAL LANDSCAPE IS SET from the opening screen of the game, with the game's music director Yuu Miyake vocalizing the opening to the game's distinctive theme tune. In the same way that the title screen is, in its essence, an abstraction of the game itself—roll ball, collect thing—the soundtrack that plays over that title screen is a distillation of the more fleshed-out soundtrack to come.

From that opening screen up through the tunes that accompany you as you grow large enough to consume continents, the music is as crucial to the game as the katamari and the objects it absorbs.

Katamari Damacy's playful, vocally driven soundtrack stands in stark contrast to other game soundtracks released that year. "2004 was the year that brought us a slew of generic and unmemorable game scores, dull and bereft of life, happiness, and color," game composer Ryan Ike told me in an interview. "From the bored-sounding metallic tones of *Doom 3* to the grody butt-rock of *Prince of Persia: Warrior Within*, game soundtracks seemed like they'd given up on giving players music they could hum along to, identify with, or even remember. Even the standouts like *Metal Gear Solid 3* gave you more of what you expected: bombastic orchestral pieces or ambient soundscapes which, even when expertly done, didn't have anything new to offer."

The *Katamari* creative team felt the same way. "The game music of the latter part of the 90s had not been very memorable," Miyake said in an interview with Video Game Music Online (VGMO). "All of this unmemorable music might be fine for its purpose, but I wanted to have something like the iconic music of the past, where just hearing it brought back memories of the game and made you want to play it again. In corporate language, I suppose you could call it a selling point."

Miyake drew deeply from the game's concept for inspiration—as well as from his own memories of the soundtracks of games he'd played when he was young.

"[W]hen I was in the 6th grade […] Harumi Hosono-san of [Yellow Magic Orchestra] released the world's first video game soundtrack, an album called *Video Game Music*," Miyake remembered in the VGMO interview. "The one I listened to until it wore out, though, was the musically superior *The Return of Video Game Music*. In the 80s, none of the music that I liked was popular, so I listened to and sought out video game music until I entered college."

He noted that his collaboration with Takahashi on *Katamari* was a smooth process because they shared the same philosophies. "At that time he and I were in the extreme minority, holding the artistic position on various matters, and we saw eye to eye," he said in the interview.

To create the soundtrack, Takahashi and Miyake recruited several in-house video game composers who had worked on such games as *Soulcalibur* and *Tekken Tag Tournament*: Akitaka Tohyama, Yoshihito Yano, Yuri Misumi, Hideki Tobeta, and Takahashi's wife, Asuka Sakai.

Takahashi and his team wanted interesting and innovative music to match the game they were making. The approach to the music for his game was similarly unconventional, guided by a strong central vision: Find interesting artists, give them loose instructions, and then allow them to do what they do best.

First, the team decided that rather than an all-instrumental score, the soundtrack would be composed entirely of songs with vocals. Miyake spoke out strongly about the choice for this direction to VGMO:

[F]rom my experiences in a band in college (I was young, so my punk spirit helped as well), I had come to dislike following the past as-is, and gained a passion for creating things that retained a method while breaking taboos, that expanded boundaries and felt different, but were still good. Around that time, an idea had come up in conversations between Keita Takahashi and myself that the absolute best way to undertake creative work is to deny the present. You could call it a dialectical approach… I think that was why we arrived at the concept of an all-vocal score.

They also wanted unconventional singers for their unconventional soundtrack. In a 2009 blog post by Kazuhito Udetsu, Miyake noted that the team deliberately sought out artists who hadn't appeared in the charts for some time. "Since [...] *Katamari Damacy* was originally only released in Japan, we wanted Japanese singers who were well-known in Japan but nobody had heard from in awhile for whatever reason," he said.

Many of the songs feature vocals from well-known J-pop singers and anime voice actors, including vocalist Masayuki Tanaka—known for the soundtracks of superhero shows like *Ultraman* and *Kamen Rider*—1980s pop idol Yui Asaka, and renowned *enka* singer Nobue Matsubara.[2]

"It was a tricky decision," Takahashi told me, referring to how they might apply their small budget to finding talent. "Some of [the singers] used to be popular around ten years ago, or very popular but in niche markets or to fans. I'm not saying they are not great artists—actually, they are super great. They were just not popular in that Japanese music market."

The composition of the music was somewhat freeform.

"The music of *Katamari Damacy* was created in an environment which fostered creativity and excitement for everyone involved," Miyake told Original Sound Version in 2009. "An interesting note is that [Takahashi] didn't give us any detailed directions regarding sound design. We were able to create the music freely as we saw fit. In fact, we worked closely with the director, graphics team, and movie team to stimulate each other creatively during the production of the game."

On the process, Takahashi said, "I had some keywords to make lyrics to composers. My memory is not perfect but I guess it was like 'rolling,' 'roll up,' 'prince,' 'katamari,' 'make a star,' et cetera. It turned out to nicely relate to gameplay."

---

2 *Enka* are sentimental ballads performed with traditional and nostalgic themes.

The result is an eclectic soundtrack that combines elements of kitschy pop genre *Shibuya-kei* with samba, jazz, and thematic inspirations drawn from traditional electronic video game music.

"I have kinda mixed feelings about music as a game designer because I know that I couldn't make a fun enough game with only actual gameplay," Takahashi said, laughing. "I definitely think *Katamari* didn't have a chance at being popular or a cult favorite without its music."

And a cult favorite it became. The game's soundtrack won both IGN's and GameSpot's "Soundtrack of the Year 2004" awards, and was nominated in 2005 for "Outstanding Achievement in Original Musical Composition" at the 8th annual Academy of Interactive Arts and Sciences Interactive Achievement Awards. The soundtrack was also released in Japan as an album called *Katamari Fortissimo Damacy*. In the years since, *Katamari* has appeared regularly on lists of the greatest video game soundtracks of all time.

With new games in the Katamari franchise came new, lauded additions to the its musical universe. "Katamari on the Swing," from 2006's *We Love Katamari*, won Best Original Vocal/Pop Song at the 4th Annual Game Audio Network Guild awards in that same year. In 2009, with the release of the third game in the series, *Katamari Forever*, came yet another album: *Katamari Damacy Tribute Original Soundtrack: Katamari Takeshi*, which featured new, fresh remixes of many of the series's favorite songs, and completed what Miyake considers the "trilogy" of Katamari albums.

But rarely has a soundtrack so perfectly captured the spirit of the game it accompanies as the soundtrack to the original *Katamari*. By incorporating a variety of genres and crafting catchy pop songs, the artists ensured that there's something on the soundtrack to appeal to nearly everyone's tastes. But this is coincidental, rather than a deliberate appeal to broadness.

When the team focused on their specific tastes and artistic vision, they created product that *they* loved. Paradoxically, this "selfishness" is necessary to make art with a chance of being beloved by many. To please others, you have to first please yourself.

KATAMARI
UNTRANSLATED

Saluton! Do you know Esperanto?
Maybe We'll invent a Cosmic Esperanto.

—The King of All Cosmos

BETWEEN EACH LEVEL, players see cutscenes about the Hoshino family—pastel, blocky figures with square-shaped heads—who live in a quaint world filled with nostalgic imagery.

As the first cutscene begins, young Michiru and her brother Mutsuo are watching a superhero show on TV when their mother comes in to tell them it's time to go. A breaking news report interrupts the program: The stars have vanished from the sky, and no one knows why.

The children ask their mother what's going on, but their mother dismisses them, saying that "things like that just don't happen." They pile into a cab and head to the airport, where they hear another news report. "The night sky is showing signs of recovery," the newscaster says, but the cause is still unknown.

As the constellations get rebuilt, Michiru can sense what's happening. "Oh! I feel it. I feel the cosmos!" she says.

On the plane, Mutsuo is gazing out the window. The King of All Cosmos is looming over the Earth, casting a massive shadow. Mutsuo points, his eyes huge, unable to speak. But the children's mother is absorbed in other matters and doesn't notice the King, only noting that they're almost at their destination. "I know I saw that huge guy," the boy says, confused.

Having arrived and deplaned, the family looks through a pair of binoculars at the faraway rocket launchpad where their astronaut father is awaiting takeoff. They board a bus for the space center, and a massive katamari rolls by in the background with a rumble.

At the space center, Mutsuo says he wants to be an astronaut. They look for their father, who runs over to them, telling them that the launch has been called off because the Moon has disappeared. Finally, as she scans the sky through an observatory telescope, the mother sees the stars disappearing from the sky, finally believing what's happening, although she seems remarkably calm about it. The children clamor for a look.

Finally, in the last cutscene, the King tosses your katamari into the sky, forming the new Moon. The

King is exhausted, he says, but the sky is complete. He also notes just how much the Prince has grown in his adventure. Well, at least one centimeter taller.

The credits roll. But the story isn't over yet.

After a bit of dancing in front of the sun, the King and Prince soar through the universe, looking at different planets, some with dinosaurs, some with super-futuristic space cities.

The game tells you your final diameter, and how many objects you rolled up. You get a view of all your Cousins, standing in a circle on their mushroom planet, holding hands.

And finally, as the staff credits scroll on the screen, you roll a small moon across the surface of the Earth, picking up individual countries along the way as a mournful but triumphant tune plays.

But wait! The Hoshino family are still there! They stand on the surface of the Moon as Mutsuo throws up his arms excitedly. "Wow… we all got rolled into the katamari and now we're on a lunar family vacation," he says. "The stars sure are pretty."

And the final screen: "That's it!"

Why the focus on this family as the narrative center of the world of *Katamari Damacy*, even though the player is acting as the Prince and speaking to the King throughout?

"I just needed a different perspective to observe that world," Takahashi told me. "To show how, even though the puzzle is rolling the katamari, [the Hoshinos are] the ones being rolled up. It's not serious, just funny. But still kind of important to have that other view."

He elaborated: "I wanted to make a game based on actual life, not fantasy or sci-fi. *Katamari* is based on actual life. I just didn't like the idea of creating a video game to solve frustration in general, like an FPS [first-person shooter]. FPSes are good at relieving frustration. This game can provide us with a nicer way."

"So I made cutscenes," he said. "I could tell a story about the Prince, or the King's story, like a sequel. But for the initial game I needed to tell stories about ordinary people's lives. Because what I wanted to tell was that the *Katamari* idea was super simple. Rolling a ball and sticking to everything. Ideally everyone can think about that idea to change your perspective. If you see a different viewpoint, maybe you don't get frustrated [by the world's troubles], and that stays with you for all your life."

•

In *Katamari*, the television is ever-present.

In any level where a television is present, it's broadcasting footage of you and the katamari you're currently rolling, as if a news camera is following you around, reporting on your every move. And knowing that the news reporters are looking for an explanation about the missing stars, it makes sense that they would seize on the appearance of a miniscule creature from another planet and his strange lumpy contraption.

But in the Hoshino household, the TV arrives even earlier. Before you and your katamari have been spotted by the family, the kids are already glued to the TV, which is showing a superhero program from a specific genre known as *tokusatsu*.

The show appears only briefly in the game, but its presence is an important nod to a genre that influenced both the game's attitude and its visual style.

"When you think *tokusatsu*, a lot of people instantly leap to Japanese superheroes à la Sentai [e.g. Power Rangers], Ultraman, and Kamen Rider," voice actor and Japanese pop culture writer Mike Dent told me in an interview. "But it really pertains to anything that has to rely on special effects. So something like Star Wars, which is highly reliant on visual effects work to tell its story, is also technically *tokusatsu*. But over the years, even though *tokusatsu* literally means 'special effects,' it's since become associated with those same [Japanese] hero shows."

The genre can be traced to the monster movies of the 50s and 60s, especially to the original *Godzilla* (1954) and other monster films, and evolved throughout the 60s, spawning other sci-fi/monster series like Ultraman (originally billed as a "special effects fantasy" show).

"But then the 70s came [...] and suddenly, *tokusatsu* wasn't all about the special effects anymore," Dent said. "It started to be focused more on the bright, colorful, exploding heroes on every network. Some would call this the golden age of *tokusatsu* because of the most innovative and iconic shows came about then."

The character on the kids' screen, known as Jumboman, is unique to *Katamari*, and reappears later in the form of several objects that can be rolled up. Its design references this nostalgic 70s Japanese superheroes aesthetic, and also harkens back to the design of one of Takahashi's university projects, the superhero with the shelf cavity in its chest.

"If you look at a lot of various movies, comics, or TV series that poke fun at or homage *tokusatsu* shows, they always relate back to that time period," Dent said. "I think it's largely because that was the era of *tokusatsu* that channeled the most imagination. In the 80s and 90s, the mainstream became more grounded, darker, and dramatic, and in the 2000s [and beyond], very few creative risks are taken for the sake of maintaining the status quo of the respective brands."

"You'll have TV shows now that will utilize CGI, yet it's the show from the 70s that had a barebones budget and that even utilized exploding action figures for a scene that ends up being more appreciated," he added.

Dent likened this preference for the less polished style of production to the concept of *wabi-sabi*, "the acceptance of transience and imperfection."

"In the Japanese *Spider-Man* series [a campy, goofy show similar in tone to Adam West's 1960s *Batman*], there's a scene where Spidey is trying to track down the villains," he said. "He finds a convoy of transport trucks, but if you pay close attention, it's really just the same truck over and over. With the right editing, pacing, and camera work, you end up being so enthralled that you're willing to ignore it or even laugh it off, but you'll still end up getting what is going on."

"And there are tons of these shows where maybe it's some quick editing and an exploding dummy of a monster to show someone getting killed, but you're visually provided with enough information to understand what's happening," he added. "And when you're a kid watching, that's the kind of stuff that sets your imagination on fire with excitement to fill in the blanks. The fact that it's today and we still have men in giant robot costumes fighting monsters in miniature cities speaks volumes about how intact this ideal is."

In addition to the literal reference to this era of Japanese culture, *Katamari Damacy* also embraces this philosophy of keeping things simple and exciting as a method of stimulating the imagination. By referencing nostalgia, it allows the player to revisit happy childhood memories as they engage in a childlike form of play.

But perhaps most importantly, it's this attitude that drove the creators to make this game in the first place. Because it's all presented through the lens of the Hoshino children, players get to see the world through the kids' eyes, and can hopefully take a bit of that youthful joy back outside the game and into their lives.

•

There's no mistaking the Hoshino family as anything but Japanese. From their names to their viewing habits, they are rooted in the same culture as the game's creator. The King of All Cosmos, however, has Japanese roots that may be far subtler to Western players.

Those roots are the only subtle thing about our gaudy King. While the Prince is ostensibly the main character of *Katamari Damacy*, our adorable little player character is also basically interchangeable with his same-sized Cousins. The true lord of *Katamari Damacy*, including our planet and solar system but clearly extending to much larger swaths of the universe, is the King of All Cosmos.

Visually, the King cuts quite a dashing figure. His wide, cylindrical head is resplendent with rainbow hues, wavy stripes, and flickering lights, topped by a crown. His skin is grey, and beneath his orange, triangle-shaped nose is a carefully-shaped mustache and goatee. He wears a huge ruffled collar, with a flowing purple robe, and a gold chain around his neck. His blue shirt gapes open in a wide V, revealing grey skin and a well-toned figure. His purple tights extend from waist to toe, and showcase muscled thighs and a prominent crotch bulge.

For Westerners, his outfit evokes some of pop culture's favorite glam rock performers of the 80s and 90s, such as Prince and David Bowie, with their image-conscious, gender-bending styles of dress and performance. Still, the King's character is deeply Japanese.

In a culture with rigid hierarchies and incredible social pressure to adhere to traditional behaviors associated with a particular gender, job, or role in life, acting out those traditional behaviors is equally as performative as subverting them. The book *Men and Masculinities in Contemporary Japan: Dislocating the Salaryman Doxa* describes how this can be seen in how many Japanese professions. These companies still have an "unofficial-official" uniform and set of expected behaviors, such as the dark suit and social drinking of the "salaryman," a term used for male office workers.

The closest term we have for this in Western culture is "stereotype," but in Japan these signifiers are frequently far more complex, and the Japanese language and culture accommodates these complexities. For example, in Japan, gender can be reinforced by language, or neutralized, depending on the terms of self-reference selected by the speaker, the manner of speaking, and the inflection given to words.

These complexities extend to notions of gender and sexuality as well. Japanese theater has a long tradition of all-male or all-female casts portraying roles of the opposite gender, creating what Karen Nakamura and Hisako Matsuo call "special types of asexual, agendered spaces" in which "both female and male fans, regardless of their sexual orientations, can temporarily transcend their everyday gender expectations and roles" before returning to their everyday lives. This crossing of boundaries is considered acceptable as long as it doesn't encroach on the home and family structure.

Likewise, cross-dressing and drag is heavily associated in Japanese media with homosexuality, while at the same time there exists in Japanese culture an understanding that behaviors that subvert traditional roles, including visual presentation or representing oneself as a different gender online, may be divorced from sexuality or sexual behavior.

Further, sexual behavior can be separate from the roles a person takes on in their everyday life, such as working in the office or being a part of a family. As cultural historian Mark McLelland explains, even when a sexual element is present—for example in scandals involving married politicians who engage in homosexual activity—it is "often described [in the media] as a 'play' (*purei*) or a 'hobby' (*shumi*) and does not have the same moral valency as is attributed to it in the West."

The King is ascribed with many traditionally Japanese feminine qualities, such as his desire for "fabulousness," his taste for sweets, his talkativeness, and his clear attention to personal grooming. But his role in *Katamari Damacy* is traditionally masculine: He is a creator, a leader, and a father.

The King is drawn from a character archetype common on Japanese television, one identified by critical language studies scholar Claire Maree as the *onē* ("queen") or *okama* (a slur now reclaimed by the Japanese queer community), types known for their *dokuzetsu* ("virulent tongue") and drag performance.

As Maree notes, these characters speak in a way that "often combines the genteelness of JWL [Japanese women's language] with a vitriolic wit and obscenities in much the same way as camp English and drag queen talk. […] It is a parody that employs a uniquely vitriolic and comical force in which the coupling of hyperfemininity with creative bitchiness is key."

The way the King's personality is presented can be uncoupled from the idea of his being queer himself, since he's shown to be in a heterosexual relationship. Instead, we're supposed to understand that the character's charm comes from the silliness inherent in parody. We love the King and appreciate his campiness because of how he transgresses the assigned cultural roles of masculinity, shedding light on their absurdity through exaggeration.

As in the gameplay, the sense of scale becomes important in relation to the King, too.

The opening cinematic of *Katamari Damacy* focuses mostly on the King, and everything is presented in relation to him, including our own world. The very first scene shows his massive, shadowed form rising ominously over a pastoral scene of cows grazing in a field.

The Prince is present, but he's usually next to the King or on top of him, perched on the King's knee. When the Prince is featured on his own, he's always on Earth, appearing on top of a volcano, or floating through the air wearing butterfly wings.

In contrast, the King is always in positions of control: driving a car, dropping sparkles that cause mushrooms to sprout across the landscape and fill the screen, or flying through the sky with a body literally comprised of the starry night sky.

The King's power in the game is absolute. He is a creator god with the power of life, a monarch who rules over the universe and all its inhabitants, and a patriarch within a rigid, traditional family structure.

Much of his charm lies in the fact that, although he surely means well, he's a terrible caretaker of all of those things. All of the action of *Katamari Damacy* is due to his clumsiness: While drinking, he ricocheted around the night sky, shattering all of the celestial bodies it contained.

He's somewhat apologetic about it, but his emotions don't quite map to typical human feelings.

"Yes, We were naughty. Completely naughty," he tells the Prince in the preface to the first level, completely oblivious to all the stellar destruction he has caused. "So, so very sorry. But just between you and Us, It felt quite good. ♥ Not that We can remember very clearly, but We were in all Nature's embrace. We felt the beauty of all things, and felt love for all. That's how it was. Did you see? We smiled a genuine smile. Did you see? The stars splintering in perfect beauty."

The only characters in *Katamari Damacy* with any dialogue are the King and the Hoshino family. Within that family, Michiru specifically is the one who speaks the most, although we hear from her family members and television sets nearby. She, like the King, feels a direct connection to the stars.

Michiru and the other humans' voices are portrayed by voice actors. Her refrain, "Oh! I feel it. I feel the cosmos!" has become a common quote in reference to the game, maybe because it's one of the only spoken phrases that players encounter.

The King's voice, however, is never heard—not as words, anyway.

In scenes before every level, the King stands tall against the celestial sky, his arms crossed, back straight. The Prince stands on the Earth's surface with the curve of the planet barely visible beneath his feet, but compared to the King, he's barely a speck at the bottom of the screen.

The King usually greets the Prince in a myriad of world languages, inviting his son to visit those countries, then corrects himself by saying that his son is obviously too busy to travel, since he has so much work to do cleaning up the mess on Earth. The words appear onscreen as text, but instead of a recorded voice, his audio is the sound of a record scratch, an appropriate substitute voice for a game that places so much importance on music.

Media depictions of the voice of god tend to say a lot about the artist's hopes, fears, or sense of humor.

Many films choose to cast either a child, suggesting power beneath an innocent, pure exterior, or a gravelly elder, suggesting a certain warmth, world-weariness, and wisdom. In the Kevin Smith film *Dogma*, god is played by the singer Alanis Morissette. She is mostly silent, communicating only by gesture. When she finally speaks, it's a sound too powerful for the human characters to handle, a roar that shakes the world.

The King's one-way conversations with his son say a lot about his role as the head of his family. In the world of *Katamari Damacy*, the role of monarch informs both the King's attitude toward the earth and his attitude toward his son.

The Japanese imperial family is the oldest hereditary monarchy in the world, claiming a lineage stretching back 2,600 years. After the Second World War, a law was enacted during American occupation which restricted membership in the Imperial Family to the emperor's immediate family and direct male heirs.

Most recently, this nearly led to a crisis of succession, as most of the current generation of the royal family produced daughters, who give up their royal title and membership in the family as soon as they marry a non-royal. While the crisis has been shelved with the announcement of a new imperial abdication plan, this anxiety can be felt in the few references to the monarchy contained in *Katamari Damacy*.

"Don't presume to take the escalator up to the throne just because you're the Prince," the King says, casually and a bit cruelly. It's one of many admonitions he makes to his son, critiquing his small size and the lackluster quality of his katamari.

There are also moments when the King is proud of his son, particularly when he's rolled up a huge amount of stuff, although it's sometimes a qualified compliment.

"Unbelievable," the King tells the Prince after he's rolled up a huge-sized bear. "You're amazing. We have finally been surpassed. You have surpassed your own father. This will make the finest Ursa Major ever. Sigh... We shall try harder..."

But why is he so mean to the Prince anyway?

"If he wasn't so mean, there's no game," Takahashi said. "He's an archetype, like from a Japanese television drama. The typical father in Japan is like a king: 'I decide. You do this. I don't like that.' Everyone is familiar with the type in real life, and that situation is common. But if it's in fiction, it can be kind of funny."

This is the one layer that can still be lost in translation as we view *Katamari* with Western eyes: A character who Japanese players instantly recognize as a playful spin on an old trope may instead scan to us as merely a real jerk. Luckily, even if some of the game's subtler cultural cues go unnoticed, the whimsy of *Katamari* is impossible to miss.

A DEEPER MEANING

What? You forgot your own planet?
Really? Are you serious?

—The King of All Cosmos

THE PLOT OF *KATAMARI DAMACY* naturally lends itself to interpretation. From different angles, it could be seen as a game about parent-child relationships, ecology, capitalism, and especially materialism.

As Jordan Mammo points out at Kill Screen, "*Katamari Damacy* cheerfully depicts a kind of snowballing addiction to acquisition that literally uproots the earth itself."

This observation has not escaped Takahashi, who has at times said that *Katamari* is about mass consumption. As he said in a Polygon interview, "So many things we have—do we need that? Do you need that?"

This sentiment was reflected in my own conversations with him. "People get way too used to the Earth," Takahashi told me. "They're not sensitive to how objects are precious. People treat it as just stuff, because it's cheap. But I don't think that's right."

"I'm not correct, just idealistic," he said. "But [with the game] at least people should be happy. Or at least they should smile rather than cry. At least that's what I can do, maybe. What I want to do. It's kind of worthless."

However, while Takahashi believes in environmental issues like fighting pollution and wastefulness, and speaks about them when delivering talks, that wasn't on his mind when he was developing the game.

Instead, Takahashi was after something much simpler: He wanted to make life a little more enjoyable. "I'm not trying to help people escape reality or vent their frustration," he said. "Instead of saying that playing a game is only meant to be a happy diversion, I would like to make daily life a bit more fun by giving people a nice game to play once in a while."

For Takahashi, part of that challenge is to create games that don't over-rely on violence. In the 2005 GDC postmortem, Takahashi spoke, through a translator, on the importance of non-violence in games.

Probably you might feel an atmosphere from *Katamari Damacy*, like [a] peaceful and mellow atmosphere, that represents my thought and my team's ideas. That peaceful and calm atmosphere is important. In Japan, we discussed a lot the impact of violent games. I'm not sure violence in Japan has been influenced by violent games, but it's unfortunate that video games became a criminal of that. And I was thinking, it is [possible for games to make a] positive impact [...] For example, the person who doesn't like animals all of a sudden likes to go to a zoo. Or your partner who doesn't like vegetables all of a sudden starts trying to grow some vegetables. Have we ever seen that kind of positive impact by playing fun games? If there is a bad impact from violent games, maybe we can have positive impact by playing fun games.

Takahashi also strongly believes that games are not meant to be replacements for going outside and having fun, especially for children.

"If game players enjoy and are devoted to playing *Katamari Damacy* I would be honored, but I might not be happy if people spend dozens of hours in[doors] playing the game," he said. "Ultimately, balance is important. Children would be better off playing outside. The time when you're a child is the only time you can experience [the world] as a child. You can play games when you become an adult."

Still, there is value in play for all of us, no matter what age we are. Play is about learning, gaining skill, and changing one's perspective.

The mere act of playing a game is one of bringing order to a chaotic world. You enter the game world with no knowledge of the rules, mechanics, levels, or challenges that lie ahead. The first thing a player does is test the game to understand where its boundaries lie, what they are and aren't capable of doing, and what the game allows.

"People solve puzzles because they like pain, and they like being released from pain, and they like most of all that they find within themselves the power to release themselves from their own pain," wrote Mike Selinker and Thomas Snyder in *Puzzle Craft*, a guide to creating puzzle games and challenges.

Slowly, whether it's through accumulating skills or weapons, leveling up a character to be super-strong, solving a riddle, or tidily fitting blocks into gaps between other blocks, we grow and gain mastery over the game world. Soon we know its contours thoroughly, we've collected every object within it, we've won every achievement, and we've seen its whole story. Through gameplay, we're able to release ourselves from a painful state of ignorance.

And ultimately, it is gameplay that Takahashi is most concerned with. All other themes take a backseat.

As game designer Ricky Haggett told me, "If there is commentary in *Katamari*, I think you have to look beyond the game to find it. I don't think you play

Katamari and go, 'Oh, [Takahashi] is trying to say this particular thing about the world.' I don't think that you would come to [the game] as a neutral person and say, 'It's obviously about this.' It's just about a big ball that rolls everything up."

Even if there was not originally an intentional larger metaphor to be found in *Katamari*, there is meaning to be found in the gameplay itself. *Katamari* is a curated experience that naturally calls our attention to the beauty and vulnerability of the world around us.

•

When Aidra Frazier and Ernest Leitch of Buhl, Idaho decided to get married, they wanted to elope, but their parents insisted that they have a wedding ceremony.

"We were having a ceremony for the sake of other people, in a location we weren't crazy about," Frazier told me. "That really doesn't help motivate wedding planning. At first we were joking around with different [theme] ideas, but when *Katamari* came up, it kind of spoke to us." Soon it was decided: They were having a *Katamari* wedding.

"Having a theme like that made wedding decisions easier," she added. "Colors? All of them. Music? Soundtrack. Attire? Ridiculous headpieces! What will we tell our parents? They're the ones that wanted a wedding, so they should be careful what they wish for."

The wedding received a lot of coverage on pop culture blogs, which featured photos of the hammer-shaped headpieces worn by the wedding party, the katamari-shaped cake that included renderings of the bride and groom, and the colorful paper lanterns that decorated the site.

In my interview with her, Frazier also referenced an early page of *xkcd*, a black and white webcomic by Randall Munroe featuring stick figures that often references pop culture, philosophy, physics, and love.

In the comic, a character approaches another, who is playing a video game in front of a television.

"Can you pause for a moment and help me with something?" the first figure asks.

"You know, our love is like a katamari," the second figure replies. "We travel along, rolling up more and more of the world into our shared experience, taking it and making it our own." The first figure is touched, but then is less touched as it becomes clearer the gamer isn't going to get up to help.

Over time, *Katamari*'s legacy continues to grow in strange new directions. On June 18, 2015, a Twitter bot named Katamari Collection began posting screenshots of items from *Katamari Damacy*'s collection catalog, garnering nostalgic comments and renewing appreciation for the quality of Agness Kaku's English-language localization. The bot has steadily continued its mission of "cataloguing every item from the Katamari series one at a time," and as of this writing has posted just over 3,000 items along with their descriptions.

But another recent development has ensured that the legacy of *Katamari* will not only grow in the hearts of fans, but endure into the future. In July 2012, the game was featured in the "Century of the Child: Growing by Design" exhibition at the New York Museum of Modern Art (MoMA), and again for a 2013 exhibition titled "Applied Design."

In "Century of the Child," the MoMA examined the relatively new concept of "childhood" and how it has developed since 1900, noting that "[d]esigners of the modern period have done some of their most innovative work with children in mind."

More significantly, *Katamari Damacy* is now a permanent part of the museum's collection.

"Are video games art?" wrote Paola Antonelli, senior curator at the museum's Department of Architecture and Design in a blog post about the acquisition. "They sure are, but they are also design, and a design approach is what we chose for this new foray into this universe. The games are selected as outstanding examples of interaction design—a field that MoMA has already explored and collected extensively, and one of the most important and oft-discussed expressions of contemporary design creativity."

Museum curation of video games is a fairly new development in the field of fine arts, and new techniques have been developed to add video games to collections, where each game is archived in its entirety, from its code to the console it's played on.

In the case of each game, the curator must decide how people experience the game in the exhibition setting. Is it short enough to play from start to finish, as in the case of some smaller art games? Is there a demo version available that gives a representative experience? Or does it require a guided tour and explanation, such as in the case of complicated or internet-connected massively multiplayer online (MMO) games?

And then there's the biggest question of all: What games make it into the museum's collection?

Antonelli described the process of making those choices, and what museums look for when considering a new piece.

As with all other design objects in MoMA's collection, from posters to chairs to cars to fonts, curators seek a combination of historical and cultural relevance, aesthetic expression, functional and structural soundness, innovative approaches to technology and behavior, and a successful synthesis of materials and techniques in achieving the goal set by the initial program. This is as true for a stool or a helicopter as it is for an interface or a video game, in which the programming language takes the place of the wood or plastics, and the quality of the interaction translates in the digital world what the synthesis of form and function represent in the physical one. Because of the tight filter we apply to any category of objects in MoMA's collection, our selection does not include some immensely popular video games that might have seemed like no-brainers to video game historians.

In MoMA's catalog you'll discover a short list of works tagged as "software," a category that clumps together fonts like Helvetica and Verdana, Björk's app/album *Biophilia*, and video games like *Katamari Damacy*. Some of these games are "no-brainers": *Pac-Man*, *Tetris*, *Space Invaders*, *Pong*. Along with these classics are games from a more modern canon, like *Portal*, *The Sims*, *Myst*, and *Minecraft*. A few choices might surprise video game historians. *Dwarf Fortress*? *SimCity 2000*? *Hyper Street Fighter II: The Anniversary Edition*?

Just as MoMA's small and eclectic collection is only a tiny snapshot of video game design history, it also only gives a small glimpse into Takahashi's art. A MoMA patron with no knowledge of games might see *Katamari Damacy* and marvel at this singular work from 2003. Little would they know that the game has spawned numerous sequels, spin-offs, and merchandise, none of which you'll find in the museum gift shop.

WE SELL KATAMARI

*When it gets this big, it's hard to tell what you have the most of.
My, Earth really is full of things.*

—The King of All Cosmos

IF YOU SCANNED THE SHELVES at your local big box retailer or games shop in 2004, you may have been surprised to find that there was no *Katamari Damacy* merchandise to be found anywhere.

A game this cute seemed positively destined for figurines, mugs, and plushies. And yet the only way you could get your hands on official *Katamari Damacy*-themed goods was if you had been paying attention to a small company based in Portland, Oregon called Panic, Inc.

Panic, Inc. was founded in 1997 as a Mac software company, offering an FTP client, an MP3 player, and a Usenet reader.

And for many years after the release of the game, Panic was also the only company in the world to release officially-licensed *Katamari Damacy* merchandise.

Once again, the story involves the meeting of several people with unconventional ways of looking at the world, a serious drive to create cool things, and good timing.

In 2003, Panic ran a booth at Macworld Expo, an Apple Macintosh trade show. As part of their sales promotion, they offered limited edition t-shirts that bucked the widely-mocked trend of poorly-designed, ill-fitting free swag.

The shirts had cool designs: the gradient-styled spinning wheel that users see whenever they boot up a Mac, or a small pixel version of the Panic logo. They were later sold through the Panic website.

So in 2005, when a friend of co-founder Cabel Sasser mentioned how cool it would be for Panic to make *Katamari* shirts, his first reaction wasn't *No way*. It was *Hmm, that could work*.

Sasser and the Panic crew had been fans of *Katamari Damacy* since encountering it at E3 in 2004.

"It was one of those things where somebody was like, no matter what else you see, you have to go check this weird thing out," Sasser told me in an interview. "It was clear that nobody had any idea what to do with this game. It was just sort of shoved over to the side. It was immediately obvious that it was significantly more interesting than anything else I'd seen over the last three days, and I just could not stop watching people play it."

Sasser emailed Nobuhiro "Noby" Hasegawa, president (and only employee) of Panic Japan, to see how they might approach a t-shirt licensing deal.

"I'm sure I was half-kidding, half-serious," Sasser said. "That happens a lot, where I'll daydream about something, and then I realize it's ridiculous but I've gotta get it out of my brain. So I said that to him, and he took me seriously."

Hasegawa looked up a contact at Namco Japan, and that same day, arranged a licensing meeting. He met with Takahashi and Namco's licensing liaison, Kei Umeki, and was granted permission.

"That's it. That's how it happened: Just like that," Sasser said.

After the meeting, Hasegawa described the situation to Sasser, telling him that Takahashi was "an outsider within Namco. He's a sculptor making video games. We are a software company that's somehow interested in making t-shirts. And to him, that is the correct match. That isn't our business—we're not 'the licensed t-shirt company' or whatever, and that resonated with him. It just seemed to make sense: Of course these shirts would come from this weird company that doesn't make shirts."

At the time, the only *Katamari Damacy* products that had ever been made were created for internal use at Namco: two puppets of the Prince, one a hand puppet and one a marionette.

Takahashi is "very protective of his creation," Sasser wrote in a 2007 blog post. "At the time we were speaking, Namco had huge success with their Taiko Drum Master series of video and arcade games, and the (very cute) characters and designs for Taiko Drum Master were being merchandised and printed on every possible product imaginable throughout all of Japan. It was a clear and vivid depiction of the extremes of licensing. [...] I think Takahashi saw this, and felt that the over-commercialization of his game and idea would really dilute the beauty and uniqueness of it."

Sasser had expected to create designs similar to the t-shirts the company had produced for Macworld: small, tasteful designs on carefully-chosen colorful shirts. So he was surprised by the initial designs Takahashi sent—they mostly featured animals, without many—or sometimes *any*—*Katamari* characters.

"The color combinations were totally bonkers, but awesome. I found that my job was mostly to push for slightly more boring but acceptable ones," Sasser said in the interview. "Basically we just said, 'We'll do whatever you want. Sure, we can print eight different designs. How about we do this one fuzzy?' It was that kind of collaboration."

The shirts were printed by a shop in southeast Portland and sold through the Panic website as officially-licensed merchandise. Although they eventually sold units to the web shop for Bandai Namco USA, they opted not to pursue distribution into stores.

"It was just a fun little weird hobby for us," Sasser said. "This was not like, 'We're gonna become a full-scale t-shirt company.' But honestly, it was one of the most enjoyable experiences. It couldn't have been more fun."

Sasser said that Panic still receives emails about the shirts, including a guy who wanted a source art file to create custom Lego minifigures to use as wedding cake toppers, as he had been wearing the shirt when he met his wife. "It's funny how you do something silly like that but then, as a total side consequence, this stuff is woven into people's lives, attached to memories," he said. "I'll still see random people wearing them around. They live on in the weirdest ways."

•

In the years since *Katamari Damacy*'s release, the game has spawned a number of sequels across multiple consoles and platforms, each integrating new types of gameplay while almost always maintaining the core "roll and grow" mechanic of the original game.

However, only the first two games in the series were directly overseen by Takahashi.

The first direct sequel, *We Love Katamari* (*Minna Daisuki Katamari Damashii,* stylized as "We ♥ Katamari" in the US) was released in Japan on July 6, 2005, in North America on September 20, 2005, and in Europe on February 2, 2006. This was the first time a Katamari game had an official release in the European market.

We Love Katamari features a story about fans sending letters making special requests of the Prince and King of All Cosmos, and the Prince's attempts to keep up with the demands of his adoring public. The game introduced several new objectives. In one level, you must roll a sumo wrestler over food items to prepare for and win his match. In another, you must create the snowball head of a massive snowman.

After working on *We Love Katamari*, Takahashi was uninterested in continuing to work on future sequels. Instead, he created the game *Noby Noby Boy* for the PlayStation 3 (2009) and for the iPhone (2010) before leaving Bandai Namco in 2010 after eleven years with the company.

Takahashi was ambivalent about seeing the Katamari franchise continue without him. "I can't deny the fact that people work on sequels," he told Eurogamer in a 2010 interview about his departure. "After all, it's a business. But at the same time, in the past decade or so, I've only seen most companies working on the safe side making more sequels."

We Love Katamari's reception from reviewers and fans was generally favorable. "[I]sn't *We Love Katamari* a sequel?" wrote Levi Buchanan in the *Chicago Tribune*. "Technically, yes—but it's more akin to a second chance. It's another opportunity for gamers to demand innovation and originality. [...] After buying in such small sales numbers the first time around, gamers should count themselves lucky to see Katamari again, and justly reward Namco's decision to take the risk again."

After a while, though, the decision to produce Katamari sequels became less of a risk as Katamari transitioned from "risky iconoclast" to "dependably bankable property."

In the years that followed, Bandai Namco have produced several sequels and spin-off games across various platforms, experiencing diminishing returns and less favorable reviews with each one. While most of the follow-up games stuck to the core mechanic of "roll object, grow bigger," they only offered a handful of new levels, songs, or Cousin designs at most. Worse still, many of the titles ignored the original design mission of keeping gameplay as simple as possible.

In 2006, *Me & My Katamari* (*Boku no Watashi no Katamari Damashii*) was released for the PlayStation Portable (PSP) in the US and Europe, after a December 2005 release in Japan. It was the first Katamari game for a portable system. *Me & My Katamari* told the story of the Royal Family's tropical vacation to Earth, where the King accidentally causes a tsunami to hit the nearby

Paradise Commonwealth Island. Players are tasked with picking up specific types of objects to rebuild islands for animals, such as fuel-related items to help a gorilla power a rocket ship, similar to the zodiac constellation tasks in the original *Katamari*. Unfortunately, *Me & My Katamari* asked players to roll through the same levels multiple times, with only weather or time of day changing between them.

Katamari Damacy Mobile (*Katamari Damashii Mobairu*) was released in June 2007 for Japanese mobile network NTT DoCoMo as a pre-installed game on Mitsubishi P904i mobile phones. The phones featured software called "GestureTek EyeMobile" that utilized the phone's camera to detect tilt and vibration. Users rolled the katamari around using tilting gestures only, the first time that feature had been synthesized with *Katamari's* gameplay.

A second Katamari-related mobile game was released for the launch of NTT's "DoCoDeMo Game" service, featuring a crossover between Katamari and Takahashi Meijin. Takahashi Meijin is a Japanese man who became famous in the 1980s for being able to press a game trigger button sixteen times per second, and who later appeared as a character in his own game, *Takahashi Meijin's Adventure Island* (known simply as *Adventure Island* in the West, which renames the title character "Master Higgins"). The *Takahashi Meijin and Katamari*

Damacy game featured Meijin pushing a ball made of items he had collected.

Beautiful Katamari (*Byūtifuru Katamari Damashii*) followed in the US and Japan in October 2007 on the Xbox 360. Directed by *Me & My Katamari* co-lead game designer Jun Moriwaki, *Beautiful Katamari* featured a story in which the King of All Cosmos rips a hole in the fabric of the universe while playing tennis. The Prince is sent to recreate the sun and planets of our solar system, and finally to plug the black hole.

It was the first game in the series to support high-definition displays, and had multiplayer modes that could be played over Xbox Live. It was also the first Katamari game to feature downloadable content: seven additional levels available for purchase through the Xbox Live Marketplace. The game was criticized because purchasing these levels was the only way that players could earn the "Astronomic Katamari" achievement for making a katamari over 1,500,000 km in size.

Rolling with Katamari was a November 2008 mobile release for U.S. Cellular's data subscription service Easyedge. It utilized the (non-smartphone) phones' D-pad or trackball controls, and featured isometric views of pixel art-style levels, including one set on the circuit board of the phone itself, with the Prince's katamari absorbing its chips and other electronic components. These circuit board chips are likely the smallest objects ever to be rolled up in the Katamari universe. The very next month, *Rolling* was followed by a smartphone game, *I Love Katamari*, which utilized the iPhone's tilt controls.

In March 2009, a falling block puzzle game called *Korogashi Puzzle Katamari Damacy* was released in Japan for the handheld Nintendo DSi console. Its gameplay style mimicked that of a previous Namco game, *Pac-Attack*, which was itself a descendent of games such as *Dr. Mario*. Players drop blocks into the field of play to form barriers and pathways that the Prince can follow, to roll up pieces of fruit.

Initially released for Xbox 360, *Beautiful Katamari* had been scheduled for subsequent release on the PlayStation 3 and Nintendo Wii, but development for those platforms was cancelled. As a result, Namco instead released *Katamari Forever* (*Katamari Damashii TRIBUTE*) for PlayStation 3 globally in 2009, featuring 31 levels from previous series titles and three new levels. The story is about the King of the Cosmos suffering amnesia, with players instead fulfilling the whims of a rampaging RoboKing who has destroyed the night sky, and bringing color back to the black-and-white world.

Beautiful Katamari and *Katamari Forever* offered a new Xbox 360/PS3 generation of gamers a first encounter with the series. However, much of the goodwill attained by the original two games in the series had been lost, with fans becoming rightfully skeptical of sequels that replicated the characters and aesthetics of the original without innovating on its gameplay.

As *Beautiful Katamari* was in development in 2007, the Korean developer WindySoft licensed the Katamari brand to create a massively multiplayer online (MMO) game, eventually released in 2010. In this Korean-language game, *Goehon Online* ("Katamari Damacy Online," in Korean)[3] players could gather in a large "lobby" area, where they could show off their highly-customizable Cousin avatars and accessories, or they could play in competitive "battle" modes, in which multiple people, playing in two teams, rolled up items on the same level to try and grow or to collect the most of a specific item, or to grow and crash into one another, knocking items off of the opponent's katamari.

While the original release of *Katamari Damacy* featured competitive "crash" levels, *Goehon Online*'s multiplayer mode was cooperative, with each player directing one of the two sticks to move a single katamari. The MMO team play feels like a natural extension of the original game in a way that none of the other sequels managed to achieve, and yet its release was limited to Korean players.

---

3 "Goehon" is the Korean pronunciation of the two characters that represent "Katamari Damacy" in Japanese.

A second iOS release, *Katamari Amore*, came out in 2011, which offered players the choice among three different control schemes, including tilt controls, multi-touch, or virtual dual sticks on the screen. *Amore* drew criticism when, upon its original release, there was only a single level available the game's timed mode: Additional levels had to be purchased separately.

More sequels followed: *Touch My Katamari* (*Katamari Damacy No-Vita*) for the handheld PlayStation Vita console in 2011, and smartphone games *Katamari Damacy Mobile 2* (2012), *Tap My Katamari* (2016), and *Amazing Katamari Damacy* (2017). All drew criticism for a lack of originality and a recycling of levels and music from the original games.

Tap My Katamari in particular was a rough addition to the Katamari canon. The Prince rolls a ball, while facing the right side of the screen. The player taps the screen continuously to keep the katamari rolling, and… that's it. From an animation standpoint, it appears that the katamari remains in one place, while the background scrolls behind it, bringing objects to it. Individual objects lay in the path of the katamari, which are absorbed as soon as it hits them. This type of interaction, in which all the player does is tap a screen without additional control or agency, is known as a "one-button game." TouchArcade's Shaun Musgrave wrote, "From the moment the first details on *Tap My*

Katamari were released, the overwhelming sentiment seemed to be that this game shouldn't be. [...] Seeing the brand used for a fairly blatant attempt at getting a little cash from one of the mobile flavors of the moment just doesn't seem right to some people."

The magic of the original *Katamari Damacy* is in the act of turning complexity into simplicity. A PS2 controller that could intimidate a first-time player becomes an intuitive, fluid experience. The vastness of the world's life and material culture is rolled up into a big ball that becomes a single, shining star. So there's an irony in the production of so many sequels, each a lesser shade of the spirit of joy that drove the original, with the final version requiring only the slightest touch of a fingertip, requiring no skill and offering no emotional impact.

Luckily for us, the original game still exists. The clutter of *Katamari*'s many sequels does nothing to taint the original's reputation or to stifle all our warm feeling for it. And even if they offer little else, the games' titles have a point. Katamari is beautiful. We love Katamari. I love Katamari. And I could play it forever.

KATAMARI FOREVER

All right, that's it for time. We have a meeting to go to.
We're zipping back to Space now. Royal Rainbow!

—The King of All Cosmos

THE KATAMARI BRAND HAS GOTTEN a lot of mileage since its debut in 2004, and the end result is just like the series's representative object: a big clump of stuff. Some of it is precious. A lot of it is junk. And deep inside this big amalgamation of games and creators and merch and fandom is the thing that started it all, *Katamari Damacy*.

Much of *Katamari Damacy*'s charm comes from how clearly it communicates the guiding philosophy of Keita Takahashi, a man who embraces ecstatic, childlike fun with the subversive eye of the mythological trickster. A man determined to, in his own words, "ignore the players and our companies ... [to] just try creating a game that we like," but who eschews the idea that video game makers should be worshipped as auteurs, Takahashi ended up shifting the way that a whole generation of future game-makers looked at the possibilities of game design.

Given his momentous influence on video games, it's easy to see how fans and fellow developers have positioned Takahashi as the very type of auteur he tried not to become. It's even easier to look at his bright, colorful world of space royalty and cute animals and Japanese bric-a-brac and insist that there must be some of deep secret to it all.

But there's no secret. There's no one to kill. No weighty moral decisions. No overwrought plot twists. It's just a tiny dude in an adorable wonderland, rolling and rolling along to an infectious soundtrack. And that simplicity feels just as revolutionary now as it did upon the game's release.

How remarkable, then, to consider how close the game came, multiple times, to not existing at all. At every turn, someone believed in it so strongly that it was able to survive, making its way through the gauntlet and into our homes. For me, that story of the making of the game, of the many people who brought their exceptional talents and energy together to bring it into being, is where to find human truths and meaning.

Can we maintain a sense of playfulness, caring, and punk rock dedication to our visions? Can we be responsible stewards of our wonder-filled planet and everything in it, while not taking ourselves too seriously? Can we hold onto that childlike joy that gives us permission to explore, and appreciate, and be free? The existence of *Katamari Damacy* gives us a glimpse into a world where we can.

Stripped off all the baggage it has acquired over the years, *Katamari Damacy* remains one of the most innovative games to hit video game consoles, and one of the purest examples of the joy to be found in a digital game. And more than anything else, it's that sense of joy that makes Takahashi's masterpiece so beloved. All *Katamari* wants is for us to sit, play, and have some fun. The revolutionary idea at the game's core is that play itself really is enough.

NOTES

For this book, new interviews were conducted in English with Keita Takahashi, Robin Hunicke, Cabel Sasser, Ricky Haggett, Ryan Ike, Mike Dent, and Aidra Frazier.

The book also draws upon the following talks and interviews with Takahashi, listed in chronological order:

Takahashi's talk at Experimental Gameplay Workshop (EGW) 2004, available through the Game Developers Conference's channel on YouTube: https://youtu.be/0vra5PZcgaU

"The Singular Design of Katamari Damacy," published in *Game Developer Magazine* in December 2004, formerly mirrored on Robin Hunicke's blog and currently preserved at the Internet Archive: https://bit.ly/2PxOERU

"Rolling the Dice? The Risks and Rewards of Developing Katamari Damacy," Takahashi's 2005 postmortem talk at the Game Developers Conference (GDC), available in audio format through the Internet Archive: https://bit.ly/2ML7oka

"Q & A with Keita Takahashi" at IndieCade 2008 by Paul Arzt, and edited by Margaret Robertson: https://bit.ly/2NJHyt2

"Interview: The Melancholy Of Keita Takahashi" by Simon Parkin, published on Gamasutra on November 4, 2009: https://ubm.io/2LYBgV2

"Keita Takahashi: Why I left Namco" by Wesley Yin-Poole, published on Eurogamer.net on January 11, 2010: https://bit.ly/2LU5HLN

"Everything is the Game" by Mathias Crawford, published at Kill Screen on August 9, 2011: https://bit.ly/2NadEBg

"The Making Of: Katamari Damacy" by Daniel Robson, published at Edge Online on June 16, 2014 and currently preserved at the Internet Archive: https://bit.ly/2LVGXDb

"How Katamari Became One of the Most Eccentric Games Ever," posted by the staff of *Edge* to GamesRadar on July 27, 2015: https://bit.ly/2wEmPj3

"Katamari Damacy was Way Darker Than You Thought," by Allegra Frank, published on Polygon on June 22, 2018: https://bit.ly/2PvE6Tm

Keita's Mixed Media

Background on the state of Namco and the Japanese game industry in Japan in 1999 was originally compiled by Manjiro Works Japan News. Entries from October 1999 to March 2000 are now hosted at Danny Leach's homepage: http://danny.cdyn.com/japan2000.html

Katamari Takes Shape

Footage of *Densen* was released in December 1999 in issue 2 of the Japanese CD-ROM magazine *PlayPlayPLUS*, available to members of the PlayStation Club, a paid membership service. For more on this game and original footage, see Brandon Orselli's May 26, 2014 article on *Densen* at Niche Gamer: https://bit.ly/2oBwvar

Information on Japanese game developers' tenure in the industry reported in Chris Remo's "Report: Japanese Developer Salaries Average $57,590," published at Gamasutra on March 22, 2010: https://ubm.io/2wFNHQu

The 2001 "Interview with Greg Buchner" was posted to the Gaming Intelligence Agency's site on June 6, 2001: https://bit.ly/2oAe8Tf

The Sum of Its Parts

Darius Kazemi's essay, "The Prince of Objects: Katamari and Ontology," was published on his blog Tiny Subversions in a May 4, 2012 post: https://bit.ly/2oBnApq

The 2004 GameSpy interview with Toru Iwatani is Steven L. Kent's "Katamari Damashii: The Snowball Effect," published April 8, 2004: https://bit.ly/2wFc8NX

Katamari on a Roll

GameSpot's Jeff Gerstmann's remarks on *Katamari* were logged in his "TGS 2003: Katamari Damacy Impressions": https://bit.ly/2oAmpGU

Sales figures from *Katamari Damacy*'s available through VGChartz. Figures from its first week (ending March 21, 2004) are available at https://bit.ly/2oBhYvF. Figures from its tenth week, when the Famicom Mini Series was released, are here: https://bit.ly/2C9nCi5.

"Namco Plans Big" by Anoop Gantayat, published March 9, 2004 to IGN, details Namco's marketing blitz and optimistic sales figures: https://bit.ly/2LNlOLf

The EGW's mission statement is taken from its homepage, http://www.experimental-gameplay.org, last consulted July 17, 2018.

Doug Church's comments to Gamasutra are recorded in Justin Hall's "Event Wrap-Up: Tokyo Game Show 2003," posted October 15, 2003: https://ubm.io/2CeJMzw

Darius Kazemi's memories of Takahashi's talk at EGW 2004 are recorded on his blog Tiny Subversions in a January 23, 2006 post: https://bit.ly/2wDdLv2

Reviews of the game were culled from Metacritic (https://bit.ly/2PAD60x) and are listed below in order of mention. Several of these reviews are preserved in full or in part at the Internet Archive:

- Paul Theobold of GameSpy (September 20, 2004): https://bit.ly/2LTa6hW
- Jeremy Parish of 1UP (September 20, 2004): https://bit.ly/2wEZ8r7
- Tom Bramwell of Eurogamer (June 21, 2004): https://bit.ly/2MI3gRL
- Ivan Sulic of IGN (September 16, 2004): https://bit.ly/2wCWu5G
- GameSpot (captured September 23, 2004) at the Internet Archive): https://bit.ly/2CpFEwP. (Page 2 not archived).

- Frank Provo of PSX Extreme (September 27, 2004): https://bit.ly/2MLiply
- Edge Magazine at Games Radar (April 15, 2004): https://bit.ly/2wCY8nS
- Darryl Vassar of G4 TV (October 22, 2004): https://bit.ly/2C9ONJw

Huncike's blog post about *Katamari* was posted on January 30, 2005 to her blog, now preserved at the Internet Archive: https://bit.ly/2wCkQvL

The NPD sales numbers for 2004 are drawn from Romier S's "December NPD Sales data," posted January 14, 2005 to LCVG forums: https://bit.ly/2Ce2VS7. Levi Buchanan of the *Chicago Tribune* reports the same first-month sales figure in his September 20, 2005 review of *We Love Katamari* entitled "You'll Have a Ball": https://trib.in/2wB51q6

Katamari's North American sales figures sourced from Michael Pachter's interview with GameSpot, "Bitter Medicine: What Does the Game Industry Have Against Innovation?", last updated by Brendan Sinclair on December 21, 2005: https://bit.ly/2PxTDSC

The holiday sales slump in 2005 was reported in "NPD: November Game Sales Down 18 Percent," last updated by Tor Thorsen on December 15, 2005, and available at GameSpot: https://bit.ly/2oBFLLJ

Douglas Lowenstein's 2005 "state of the industry" speech at E3 president of the Entertainment Software Association is preserved at the Internet Archive: https://bit.ly/2wDbzDD

Katamari Nah-Nah

Chris Greening's "Yuu Miyake Interview: Katamari Sound Director Goes Freelance" was first posted to Video Game Music Online (VGMO) on December 1, 2012: http://www.vgmonline.net/yuumiyakeinterview/

Bandai Namco games producers Kazuhito Udetsu's "Katamari Forever – The Music" was posted to PlayStation. Blog on June 22, 2009, and is preserved at the Internet Archive: https://bit.ly/2CdVfPL

Jayson Napolitano's "Katamari Music Maestro: Yu Miyake Interview" was posted to Original Sound Version (OSV) on December 15, 2009: https://bit.ly/2wC5Crq

Katamari Untranslated

Men and Masculinities in Contemporary Japan: Dislocating the Salaryman Doxa, edited by James E. Roberson and Nobue Suzuki, was first published by Routledge in 2003. Karen Nakamura and Hisako Matsuo's "Female Masculinity and Fantasy Spaces: Transcending Genders in the Takarazuka Theatre and Japanese Popular Culture" is included as chapter four of this volume.

Mark J. McLelland's *Male Homosexuality in Modern Japan: Cultural Myths and Social Realities* was first published by Routledge in 2000.

Claire Maree's "The Perils of Paisley and Weird Manwomen: Queer Crossings into Primetime J-TV" appeared in *Multiple Translation Communities in Contemporary Japan*, edited by Beverley Curran, Nana Sato-Rossberg, Kikuko Tanabe, and published in 2015 by Routledge.

A Deeper Meaning

Jordan Mammo's "How Games Like Katamari Help Us Deal with Consumerism and the Wealth Gap," was published at Kill Screen on April 8, 2013: https://bit.ly/2MLOdXp

Mike Selinker and Thomas Snyder's *Puzzle Craft: The Ultimate Guide on How to Construct Every Kind of Puzzle* was published by Sterling Publishing Company in 2013.

"Katamari" was published as the 83rd installment of *xkcd*: https://xkcd.com/83/

The feed of Twitter bot Katamari Collection, run by Twitter user @ BeachEpisode, can be found at https://twitter.com/KatamariItems.

The exhibition catalog *Century of the Child: Growing by Design, 1900-2000* was published by the Museum of Modern Art in 2012.

Paola Antonelli's "Video Games: 14 in the Collection, for Starters" was posted on November 29, 2012, to MoMA's Inside/Out blog: https://mo.ma/2m47S4p

We Sell Katamari

Cabel Sasser narrates the history of Panic's *Katamari Damacy* shirts in "Japan: Visiting Takahashi, Talking Katamari" posted to his blog Caleb's Blog LOL on March 13, 2007: https://bit.ly/2N6bUcr

Levi Buchanan's review of *We Love Katamari* was titled "You'll Have a Ball," cited earlier cited in the chapter "Katamari on a Roll."

Shaun Musgrave's review of *Tap My Katamari*, "'Tap My Katamari' Review – The Current Trend, This Tapping Craze," was piublished at TouchArcade on July 1, 2016: https://bit.ly/2oCqw5s

ACKNOWLEDGMENTS

Thank you to Keita Takahashi for generously answering all of my questions, including the silly ones like whether the Prince is wearing purple pants or if it's his legs that are purple. (It's his legs.)

Thank you to the whole Boss Fight crew. This series wouldn't happen if it weren't for the Herculean efforts, thoughtful insights, meticulous research, and careful editing of Gabe Durham and Michael P. Williams, and I'm grateful for the opportunity to be a part of it all. Thanks also to cover designers Ken Baumann & Cory Schmitz, reader Cameron Daxon, copyeditor Ryan Plummer, proofreaders Joseph M. Owens & Nick Sweeney, and layout designer Chris Moyer.

Extra special thanks to Robin Hunicke, who helped immeasurably, from her original blogs about the earliest *Katamari Damacy* release news to insights about the role of play in games today.

Thank you to all of my interview subjects for the gifts of your time, insight, and excitement.

Thank you to Ricky Haggett, for his support, proof-reading, and thoughtful feedback and encouragement from the very beginning of this project.

Extra thanks to Andy Baio, Andy McMillan, and everyone at the XOXO Outpost for creating an amazing, supportive community that allowed this book to come into being.

Thanks to Darius Kazemi for help with publishing and writing advice, and the early observations about *Katamari* at the GDC Experimental Gameplay workshop which helped paint the picture so clearly.

Thank you to Elizabeth Simins and Felix Kramer for their emotional support and belief in this book and in me.

Thanks to Cabel Sasser and all the lovely folks at Panic for your friendship and for revealing a totally unique angle of the *Katamari* story, one which I still find pretty amazing. And for letting me touch the Prince puppets and custom iPod.

Thanks to Kazuya Iwata for help with translation.

Thanks to Justin Hall for our conversation about attending the Tokyo Game Show and the first appearance of *Katamari*.

Thanks to Paul Reynolds and Michael Keith for pointing me in the right direction when I was learning about the early development of the PlayStation 2.

Thank you to Fernando Ramallo for chatting with me about level design and all things cute.

Extra thanks to Nora Ryan and Jeffy Denight for keeping all the plates spinning.

Thanks Mink for the long-distance emotional support. I miss you.

Thanks to Rumpus House and House House for giving me somewhere to lay my head.

Thank you to Naomi Alderman for the discussion of what it's like to be a woman in writing and advice on what name to put on the cover of the book.

Thanks to all my friends who love games, puzzles, stories, and mysteries, and especially giving those things as gifts to others through their own work: Robin Baumgarten, Jerry Belich, Chris Bell, Alan Hazelden, Albert Kong, Jessica Lachenal, Mike Lazer-Walker, Lee Shang Lun, Richard Lemarchand, Nadya Lev, Johnnemann Nordhagen, Carolyn Petit, Jake Roberts, Josh Scherr, Kevin Simmons, Gabe Smedresden, Henry Smith, Nick Suttner, and Doug Wilson.

Thank you to everyone who's supported this book, backed the Boss Fight Kickstarter, chatted with me on Twitter, and shared their excitement about *Katamari Damacy* with me at an event. I love seeing people's eyes light up when they talk about this game, and I hope I've done it justice.

Thank you to anyone I've inadvertently left out for forgiving me for my terrible lapse.

And above all, thank you to my partner Jey Biddulph, for not only tolerating my many projects, but for joining me in them enthusiastically, right by my side, every time.

SPECIAL THANKS

For making our third season of books possible, Boss Fight Books would like to thank Maxwell Neely-Cohen, Cathy Durham, Edwin Locke, Mark Kuchler, Ken Durham, alraz, Adam B Wenzel, Sam Grawe, Jared Wadsworth, Sean Flannigan, Angus Fletcher, Patrick Tenney, Joshua Mallory, Brit W., Tomio Ueda, Joel Bergman, Sunjay Kelkar, Joe Murray, David Hayes, and Shawn Reed.

ALSO FROM
BOSS FIGHT BOOKS